Do It Again, Lord

Do It Again, Lord

*A Study of Acts 1 to 4
and Its Meaning for Today*

by

Randal Earl Denny

Beacon Hill Press of Kansas City
Kansas City, Missouri

All scripture quotations unless otherwise designated are from the *New International Version of the New Testament* (NIV), © 1973 by the New York Bible Society International. Permission to quote from the following copyrighted versions is acknowledged with appreciation:

New English Bible (NEB), © The Delegates of the Oxford University Press and The Syndics of the Cambridge University Press, 1961, 1970.

The Living Bible (TLB), © 1971 by Tyndale House Publishers, Wheaton, Ill.

The Bible: A New Translation (Moffatt), copyright 1954 by James A. R. Moffatt. By permission of Harper and Row, Publishers, Inc.

Dedication

To my wife's parents,
Roy and Bea Gladden
More than defenders of the faith,
they are demonstrations of it,
making many homesick to know God.

Contents

Contents

Foreword

I predict that you will have trouble with this book written by Randal Earl Denny! You'll have trouble laying it down! There's a fresh surprise on every page. Very simply, yet profoundly, the author has taken us back to the "early days" of the Christian Church.

The scriptural setting is the first four chapters of the Book of Acts. We are given a ringside seat on the great events of the closing days of Christ's ministry and the mighty transformations wrought in the lives of Christ's followers after the coming of the Holy Spirit on the Day of Pentecost.

As the pastor of the "mother church" in Los Angeles, Randal Denny has known something of the joy and enthusiasm created by those early pioneers of a new denomination. He expresses his hunger to see "that brokenness, freshness, and radiance" reproduced in the church today. He declares, "To the Early Church, the Holy Spirit was no puzzle. He was a dynamic power and presence, the heartbeat of their faith! Without the Spirit of God controlling within, religion is simply a demand without a dynamic."

In this book there are sermon suggestions galore, pertinent quotations, illuminating illustrations, and challenging appeals to present-day Christians to return to the "normalcy of Pentecost."

Do It Again, Lord will touch a responsive chord in each of our lives that, as Christian believers, we may experience fresh evidences of the power, the love, and the spontaneity of the presence of the Holy Spirit in our day.

—GEORGE COULTER
General Superintendent

Preface

An old man was observed kneeling at the grave of William Booth, Commander-in-chief of the Salvation Army. God had worked mightily through that great compassionate heart whose burden was lost souls. As he labored in the slums of sprawling cities, the fire of the Holy Spirit swept through the souls of men—seeking, saving, sanctifying, and sustaining! And now a lone figure knelt in remembrance and gratitude. His eyes were closed, his hands clasped in earnest, and his lips were moving. A spectator moved closer and overheard the man's heart cry: "Do it again, Lord! Do it again!"

As a pastor leading his people through the opening chapters of the Book of Acts, I have been deeply moved by the unveiling of the Holy Spirit! He came fulfilling the promise of another Comforter. As men opened themselves to the Lordship of Jesus, He cleansed and filled and energized. Something happened at Pentecost that this old world cannot understand—or ignore! That Spirit-filled Church was set on fire with a holy enthusiasm which united the believers into a fellowship of love unequalled before then. Such a revival doesn't have to be folded into the pages of the past, locked in the diary of a deceased church.

I believe the Holy Spirit has come for such a time as ours! There isn't anything He did in the first century that He doesn't want to do today. My heart's most pressing prayer is: "Do it again, Lord! Do it again!"

—RANDAL E. DENNY

Acknowledgments

The wonderful congregation of Los Angeles First Church of the Nazarene has given encouragement and inspiration to me as preacher and pastor. They have expected thorough preparation and responded to it. This warm and loving people have never looked upon their pastor as a "jack-of-all-trades," but as a proclaimer of God's Word. With David of old, I say: "The lines are fallen unto me in pleasant places; yea, I have a goodly heritage" (Ps. 16:6, KJV).

The teamwork of a loyal staff has provided me with the opportunity of living with the books and The Book. Clarence Crites, Dr. Victor Peters, Ron Benefiel, Oziel Flores, David Kwon, and Randy Benefiel—the last names sound different, but we really are brothers!

Appreciation is hereby expressed for permission to quote from copyrighted materials as follows:

Beacon Hill Press of Kansas City: Roy E. Carnahan, *Creative Pastoral Management;* Milo L. Arnold, *The Christian Adventure;* Fletcher Clarke Spruce, *When God Comes;* Mendell Taylor, *Every Day with the Psalms; Beacon Bible Commentary.*

The Westminster Press: William Barclay, *The Promise of the Spirit;* William Barclay, *God's Young Church.*

Abingdon Press: E. Stanley Jones, *The Way to Power and Poise:* E. Stanley Jones, *Growing Spiritually;* George Arthur Buttrick, editor, *The Interpreter's Bible,* Vol. 9.

Fleming H. Revell Company: William P. Barker, *They Stood Boldly;* Charles W. Colson, *Born Again.*

Stein and Day Publishers: Ernst G. Beier and Evans G. Valens, *People Reading.*

Inter-Varsity Press: Howard A. Snyder, *The Problem of Wine Skins*.

Harper and Row, Publishers: Howard Butt, *The Velvet-Covered Brick*.

Harper and Brothers: William Barclay,*The Mind of Jesus;* Halford E. Luccock, *Marching off the Map*.

Vision House Publishers: Ray C. Stedman, *Birth of the Body*.

Any active pastor is kept busy reading, underlining, tearing out clippings, taking notes—all a vital part of the search for ideas. Unfortunately, over a period of time, as he digests much material, it is possible that original sources are forgotten. Good quotes and good ideas have a way of becoming a part of one's own thinking processes. If I have overlooked original sources without notation, please forgive. The message of the Book of Acts doesn't belong to me only, but for all.

—R. E. D.

CHAPTER 1

Charter for the First Church

Acts 1:1-8

Since Jesus was the best photograph God ever had taken, the coming of Christ brought new revelation and perspective to our view of God. The Old Testament describes Christ as One who is to come. The New Testament exists to say Christ has come. The Old Testament portrays God as transcendent—over us. The New Testament message is God as immanent—in us. The Old Testament underscores God as Almighty, but the New Testament as Father. The major concept of God in the Old is His holiness, but the major theme of the New Covenant is His love. The total biblical message centers on God's holy love!

The Gospels describe God's holy love at work through the life and ministry of Jesus. The Book of Acts tells of God's holy love working through the Church by the empowerment of the ministry of the Holy Spirit. Acts is the companion volume to the Gospel of Luke; it is a second volume of a story which has no ending!

The author is Luke the physician, the only Gentile writer of the New Testament. As a traveling companion to

Paul, he was probably the apostle's attending physician. His medical knowledge and interests can be detected in his writings. William Sanford LaSor noted: "In 1882 W. K. Hobart published *The Medical Language of St. Luke,* in which he attempted to prove that some 400 terms in the Gospel and Acts were 'medical terms' that only a physician would know."[1]

Luke is considered the best historian of his era, as well as the best literary writer of the New Testament. His works are written in the finest Greek.

Both his Gospel and the Acts Luke addressed to a man named Theophilus, meaning, "loved of God." Nothing is known of him; perhaps he was a young Christian. It is certain, however, that he must have shared his letter from Luke with the Early Church, and we are richer for it.

The first chapter of Acts is like an intermission between acts of a drama. It is more of a transition from Luke's Gospel than a preface to the Book of Acts. Acts 1:1-8 contains Jesus' charter for First Church, the mother church in Jerusalem. In these verses is the reason for its existence, the agenda for the church, and the overview of its mission. Here is Jesus' inaugural address before going to the right hand of the Father. It is His keynote message to His disciples outlining the course of action. Jesus, the Nazarene, mandates First Church to carry on His work; the charter of operation.

Today, as in the 1st century, we face a secularized society. Persecutions to Christians around the world are more widespread than in the 1st century. Like the 1st century, our world is full of restlessness and despair; its heart is empty. In spite of many similarities between the 1st century and the 20th, "the major difference between the

---

1. William Sanford LaSor, *Church Alive* (Glendale, Calif.: Regal Books Division, G/L Publications, 1972), p. 20.

two centuries is that the virile, growing church of today must contend not only with a secularized society, but also with a secularized church."[2]

One should be open to Jesus' charter for First Church and come back to its basic precepts.

Jesus Confirmed the Proofs of the Resurrection

Luke wrote: "After his suffering, he showed himself to these men and gave many convincing proofs that he was alive. He appeared to them over a period of forty days and spoke about the kingdom of God. On one occasion, while he was eating with them, he gave this command: 'Do not leave Jerusalem, but wait for the gift my Father promised'" (Acts 1:3-4).

Luke stresses the first historical fact upon which the Church must build—the resurrection of Jesus. Jesus is alive! He showed himself to His men and convinced them, even against their doubts! This truth was not a ghost story or an hallucination. Men don't face martyrdom for a myth. The Book of Acts cannot be explained on the basis of who Jesus *was*. It only makes sense on the basis of who Jesus *is!* His life and ministry still go on today!

Pastor Ray Stedman told his congregation: "A certain man today who calls himself the Messiah has been announcing that he is the fulfillment of the predictions of the return of the Messiah to earth. He is causing quite a stir among people who are easily influenced by this type of fraud. Whenever I hear of someone like this, my first question is, 'Has he risen from the dead?' I'm not interested in any Messiah who hasn't risen from the dead!"[3]

---

2. Ray C. Stedman, *Birth of the Body* (Santa Ana, Calif.: Vision House Publishers, 1974), p. 9.

3. *Ibid.,* p. 15.

Luke lists a few proofs from the disciples' firsthand experience.

First, "He [Jesus] appeared to them over a period of forty days" (Acts 1:3). Stedman writes, "From this word for 'appear' we get our word, *ophthalmia*, which means literally, 'the eyeball.' In the modern vernacular, these disciples 'eyeballed' Jesus for forty days!"[4]

Second, "He [Jesus] . . . spoke about the kingdom of God" (Acts 1:3). His men conversed with Jesus for 40 days. They could all agree on what they heard—matters concerning the kingdom of God!

Third, "On one occasion, while he [Jesus] was eating with them, . . ." (Acts 1:4). Stedman adds, "They actually saw the food disappear. It must be terribly hard to get an hallucination to eat!"[5] Jesus was performing the normal functions of One who was alive and well!

Our faith doesn't look back to a dead past. A living Christ is our present reality! The hunger of the heart is not for the knowledge of the ancient acts of God, but for fellowship with the living Lord for today and tomorrow! As Jesus Christ, risen from the dead, engaged in fellowship with His disciples for 40 days, He desires to have such a relationship with His disciples today.

Jesus Commanded the Promise of the Father

Luke recorded: "On one occasion, while he was eating with them, he gave them this command: 'Do not leave Jerusalem, but wait for the gift my Father promised, which you have heard me speak about. For John baptized with water, but in a few days you will be baptized with the Holy Spirit" (Acts 1:4-5).

---

4. *Ibid.*, p. 16.
5. *Ibid.*

The second historical fact upon which the Church builds its charter is the fulfillment of the promise of the Father. What Jesus commands in Acts 1 is completed reality in Acts 2. Jesus commanded, "Do not leave Jerusalem, but wait for the gift my Father promised." He means literally, "Stick around in Jerusalem!" Anything done for the Kingdom without the anointing of the Holy Spirit is useless anyway. Wait for the coming of the Holy Spirit as the Father promised! Such a promise is completed in men; it is realized not by striving, but by receiving!

One cannot do His work without His Spirit. No longer does the Christian have to wait for the Spirit to come—He is here! However, one must prepare his heart by being open to the Holy Spirit. If one has not yet allowed himself to be Spirit-filled and Spirit-controlled, he must wait until he has given Him full possession of his heart. Until then a person's plans and programs will bear no fruit.

William Barclay put it well:

It is surely obvious that God cannot speak to us unless by listening we give Him a chance to speak. God cannot give us His gifts, especially the gift of His Spirit, unless we open ourselves to these gifts. That is what real prayer does; but it must be remembered that the prayer which finds God is one of the most strenuous activities which the spirit of man can undertake. Albert Edward Day, in his book *Existence Under God,* describes this true prayer: "It is not merely a flash of Godward desire, but the passionate fervour of a whole self that pants to know God and His will above all other knowing. It is not a hurried visit to the window of a religious drive-in restaurant for a moral sandwich or a cup of spiritual stimulant, but an unhurried communion with God who is never in a hurry. It is not merely the expression of a transient mood of dependence or loneliness, but the consistent cry of one who seeks to perceive and express the Ultimate Beauty. It is the antithesis of dilly-dally devotions, drowsy murmurs

19

from a pillow where sleep lies in wait, the lazy lisping of familiar phrases. . . . It is the find-or-die outreach of the soul for God."[6]

Just as Jesus Christ was the promise of the Old Testament, the Holy Spirit is the grand promise of the New Testament. He is the promise of the Father to each person who is His child. Christians have a claim on the Holy Spirit because God has promised. He cannot lie! God's promise will satisfy all one's need for spiritual life and power. His promise will be given in sufficient supply. God says, "I will pour out my spirit unto you" (Prov. 1:23, KJV). The promise of the Spirit is all-inclusive—every believer of Christ is eligible to receive Him. However, one must permit the Holy Spirit to take absolute control—which He does only in response to full surrender. How do we permit Him to take control?

First, acknowledge Christ in you. He who is resident in you awaits the opportunity to be president in you!

Second, ask Him to take complete control, to take away everything that makes Him sad, to fill you with His powerful Spirit.

Third, act upon His promise by faith. Thank God that He has done what He said, that you are His to fill and control, and then walk by faith, believing God's promise is complete.

Samuel Chadwick testified:

I received the gift of the Holy Spirit. I was led in ways I did not know, for I had hardly so much as heard that such an experience was possible. . . . Twelve of us began to pray . . . and the answer came. . . . God led us to Pentecost. The key to all my life is in that experience. It awakened my mind as well as cleansed my heart. It gave me a new joy and a new power, a new love

---

6. William Barclay, *The Promise of the Spirit* (Philadelphia: The Westminster Press, 1960), p. 47.

and a new compassion. It gave me a new Bible and a new message. Above all else, it gave me a new intimacy in the communion and ministry of prayer; it taught me to pray in the Spirit.

We cannot and must not ignore Christ's command to wait upon and seek the gift of the Holy Spirit. Having trusted in traditions, fine buildings, great fellowship of the saints, graciously executed programs—we must fall on our knees in total dependence upon the mighty power of the Holy Spirit. Without Him all is lost; with Him is sure victory in fulfilling our mission and calling. Admit to God and oneself that the secularized church has nothing to offer a spiritually starved world. Let Jesus be more than a patron saint; let Him be the Lord and Master!

Jesus Commended the Power of the Holy Spirit

Jesus announced, "But you will receive power when the Holy Spirit comes on you" (Acts 1:8). According to the central theme of the Book of Acts, the life of Jesus is to continue *in* His Church. Acts 1:8 relates that the Church is to be empowered to live Christ's life through the Holy Spirit. It is the keynote of the whole Book, the charter of the Church.

When the Holy Spirit comes, the believer will receive power—the Greek word, *dynamis*. The Church is to be a dynamic community, energized not by human power, but by the Spirit. Jesus had commissioned them to do the impossible. It would take the dynamite of the Spirit!

So much of modern church activity is lifeless and ineffective. People live crowded lives with no moments to spare, and yet at the end of the day have so little to show for it. The Spirit is not given room to invade and energize life; still nothing can take His place! Without Him, the finest buildings are but monuments, the most comprehen-

21

sive organization but a lifeless parade, the most brilliant and winsome leadership cannot guide beyond human effort. However, when God's people are empowered by the Holy Spirit, even inadequate buildings can be used to the glory of God, a church regardless of location or size can fulfill God's mission, and will discover its own leadership with vision and wisdom through the Spirit.

When a man sees the battery of his car is disconnected, he doesn't waste time trying to solve the problem by wiping the headlights or getting more padding for the seats. His car will never function until it is connected to its source of power! Let the church turn from easy busy-work and get herself connected to the source of heaven's Spirit power.

Jesus Charted the Program of the Church

The Master said to His men: "But you will receive power when the Holy Spirit comes on you; and you will be my witnesses in Jerusalem, and in all Judea and Samaria, and to the ends of the earth" (Acts 1:8). Pentecost is for "employment"—not "enjoyment"!

The only program the disciples had in mind at that point was seen in their question put to Jesus: "Lord, are you at this time going to restore the kingdom to Israel?" (Acts 1:6). According to the Greek text, the disciples continued asking Jesus over and over, "Are you going to restore the kingdom to Israel?" They seemed preoccupied with their own program for the future, trying to get it all plotted out on schedule. But Jesus made it clear that it was not schedules and timetables for restoration that mattered—it was power for transformation they needed! No, and He was not interested in restoring an old, imperfect kingdom. His men had not yet learned that "if anyone is in Christ, he is a new creation" (2 Cor. 5:17).

22

Jesus was sending the Holy Spirit to do something new, to create a reign of the Spirit in which men are dominated and energized by God's holy love. Those who wish to restore old forms are always in tension with those who desire to create the new.

In the year A.D. 1666, a great fire swept over London. That crazy-quilt of narrow, winding streets was burned to the ground. Some said, "Here's our chance to create a new city. Let's not restore the old."

Sir Christopher Wren, a genius in architecture, prepared a master plan for rebuilding London. St. Paul's Cathedral would be the central point, with great colonnades leading up Ludgate Hill. Parliament approved the plans—but then greedy real estate people swarmed to save their own interests. Anything new would be a threat. Sure enough, the opportunity was gone, and an old London was imprisoned back into its crooked, narrow ways—the restorers defeated the creators![7]

Thank God that the creators won against the restorers in 1776 and the United States of America was free to build its own future. But there was a strong and mighty crowd who wanted to restore the crown—even after the Revolutionary War.

In marriage something is wrong when the husband or wife is trying to restore something, a mood or emotion of past years, rather than creating a relationship which can survive in a changing world.

When religion simply looks back to the past, it ceases to make any contribution in its day. Too often, and too easily, religion tries to restore a vanished day; tries to preserve a period which truth once occupied, but has become outmoded by the years. Halford Luccock has written to

---

7. Halford E. Luccock, *Marching off the Map* (New York: Harper and Brothers, Publishers, 1952), pp. 97-98.

this problem. He believes rather than looking to the future with a daring faith,

> religion often becomes perverted into an effort for the restoration of forms. Religious institutions have fought sometimes with a blind fury to restore the world that existed in men's minds before Copernicus and Galileo, . . . before the Industrial Revolution. This mood has been satirized in the familiar lines:
>
> > *Our fathers have been churchmen*
> > *Nineteen hundred years or so,*
> > *And to every proposal*
> > *They have always answered, "No!"*
>
> One of the real dangers of Christianity at the present time is that a backward-looking nostalgia—a sentimental longing to go back and restore a familiar day that has either gone or never really existed—may be substituted for an ethical and spiritual religion. Nostalgia is a self-protective device, which constantly recurs in times of crisis as a defense against the painful horrors of thinking. It is an alluring, though futile attempt to escape the perplexities of an upset world, rather than to face the demanding task of taking basic Christian principles into the contemporary world.[8]

As Luccock further says, such religious nostalgia is a "sort of Currier and Ives religion. Its true symbol is

> *The old oaken bucket,*
> *The iron-bound bucket*

and the moss-covered sermon that hung in the pulpit. Its symbol is not a cross. . . . The Christian faith and experience have been a tremendous creating power in life and society. It may be so at this tense hour. It has sent men and women out to lay strong hands on the world in the name . . . of Jesus, because, His strong hands have been laid on them."[9]

---

8. *Ibid.*, p. 100-101.
9. *Ibid.*, p. 102.

The power of the Holy Spirit results in dynamic witnessing, changing lives from within. Witnessing in Jerusalem—the hometown; in Judea—in the whole country; in Samaria—to the enemies; and to the ends of the earth—to the heathens who have never heard of God's great grace! This is God's program for the Church of Jesus Christ. Instead of restoration of the old, the power of the Spirit gives new direction. Israel is not to wait for the nations to bring rich gifts. Christ's witnesses will go to the nations with good news—good news about Jesus. They will go in ever-widening circles!

A Spirit-empowered witness talks about Jesus: "This is what He has done for me!" Stedman points out: "The mark of a carnal church is that it loves to talk about itself. These early Christians never witnessed about *the church* at all; they witnessed about *the Lord*—what He could do, how He could work, what a fantastic Person He was, how amazing His power was, and what He could do in human hearts. The 20th-century church too often has its eyes focused on itself. But the Early Church had its eyes focused on its Lord, and for this reason it was an effective witness for Him."[10]

Nothing is more obvious in Acts than the fact the whole church accepted the Great Commission as binding upon every Christian. Jesus' parting words to the disciples were: "You will be my witnesses!" The overflow from their Spirit-filled hearts caused them to want to tell others. Warned not to continue a public testimony, Peter said: "We cannot but speak the things which we have seen and heard" (Acts 4:20, KJV). Jesus' followers don't have to be attorneys—just witnesses of His saving grace!

God's program cannot be carried out without His

10. Stedman, *Birth of the Body,* p. 21.

power. How can one know His power—the Spirit's *sanctifying* power?

First, one must be a born-again believer, trusting Christ for the forgiveness of his sins.

Second, one must have an intense desire to be filled with the Spirit. Those who hunger and thirst will be filled! One pastor, seeking the empowerment of the Spirit, cried: "I'd rather die than go back to my church without it!"

Third, one must surrender completely to the will of God.

Fourth, one must accept the Holy Spirit by faith. Jesus said: "If ye then, being evil, know how to give good gifts unto your children: how much more shall your heavenly Father give the Holy Spirit to them that ask him?" (Luke 11:13, KJV). Jesus also taught: "Whatever you ask for in prayer, believe that you will receive it, and it will be yours" (Mark 11:24). Faith accepts what God has promised.

CHAPTER 2

I Shall Return!

Acts 1: 9-11

By order of President Franklin Delano Roosevelt, General Douglas MacArthur, his family, and staff left Corregidor, the island fortress of the Philippines, during the night of March 11, 1942. Before stepping into the waiting PT Boat No. 41, MacArthur shook hands with his old friends, Major General Jonathan Wainwright and General Moore. Tersely, he said, "I shall return!"

The supreme commander of the Southwest Pacific directed the Allied operations from Australia and succeeded in halting the enemy advance. The many months of war ground on endlessly. It was an unforgettable struggle which gripped our world.

However, keeping his promise to return, General Douglas MacArthur waded ashore at Lingayen Beach, Luzon, on January 1, 1945. The Philippine Islands were liberated from the enemy. The general announced: "People of the Philippines: I have returned!"

On the Mount of Olives, Jesus spoke to His disciples—but suddenly, a cloud lifted Him out of sight! His men stood there in amazement—staring in disbelief! Two messengers appeared, clad in white—angels, perhaps. But, again, Moses and Elijah had appeared with Jesus on the Mount of Transfiguration, clad in brilliant white. Perhaps they were present when Jesus ascended into heaven! The messengers said, "Men of Galilee, why do you stand here looking into the sky? This same Jesus, who has been taken from you into heaven, will come back in the same way you have seen him go into heaven" (Acts 1:11).

By order of God Almighty, Jesus was called away from this old world. However, a divine promise was given that He will return! The integrity of God rests on the keeping of that promise! Jesus went away, but He is coming back. All the power of the enemy cannot keep Him away. He has promised: "I shall return!"

Jesus himself has said: "As the lightning comes from the east and flashes to the west, so will be the coming of the Son of Man. . . . They will see the Son of Man coming on the clouds of the sky, with power and great glory" (Matt. 24:27, 30).

What does the ascension of Jesus mean?

The Ascension of Jesus Is a Conclusion

The return of Jesus to His Father marks the conclusion to Jesus' earthly ministry. A definite close would be better than a gradual fading away, painfully withdrawing by fewer and fewer appearances. Jesus' ministry on earth was an epoch; a special period after the Resurrection that was necessary to establish the truth of eternal life. The period needed a definite ending. William Barclay noted: "Jesus could not remain for ever visibly with His disciples, . . . clearly He could not die all over again, and . . . there-

28

fore the end had to come in *glorification* and not in *dissolution.*"[1]

The Ascension is a conclusion to Jesus' earthly limitations. It is true that "Jesus is God spelled out in language we can understand." However, Paul states clearly that Jesus "made himself nothing, taking the very nature of a servant, being made in human likeness" (Phil. 2:7). Up to this point, Jesus had been confined to the limitations of physical existence. He dealt with frailties, weaknesses, exhaustions, frustrations which are a part of human existence.

Among the many implications of Jesus' earthly limitations, one of the most significant is His limitation in time and space while walking and living among men. Two thousand years ago, Jesus could not have shared the moment of desperation with that bereaved family in Los Angeles last night, and have heard the prayer for help in Hong Kong at the same time. He could not have been in several places at once. The Ascension marked the end of such limitations! As G. Campbell Morgan put it: "The days of limited service were over, the days of unlimited service were about to begin."

There just had to come a day of dividing when the Jesus of earth finally became the Christ of heaven!

The Ascension of Jesus Is an Introduction

William Barclay wrote: "In one sense the Ascension closes a chapter, but in another and an even greater sense it begins a new chapter, for the Ascension is the necessary prelude to the events of Pentecost and to the coming of the Holy Spirit. The Ascension is the necessary conclusion

---

1. William Barclay, *The Mind of Jesus* (New York: Harper and Brothers, 1960), p. 319.

of one part of Jesus' ministry and the equally necessary introduction to the next and even greater part of that ministry."[2]

The Ascension is an introduction to Jesus' enthronement. It is a celebrated moment when God welcomed Jesus back to His throne of glory. He ascended into heaven to begin His reign of power. After the humiliation and shame of the Cross and the triumph of the Resurrection, Jesus took His rightful place beside God the Father. The author of Hebrews explains: "The Son is the radiance of God's glory and the exact representation of his being, sustaining all things by his powerful word. After he had provided purification for sins, he sat down at the right hand of the Majesty in heaven" (Heb. 1:3).

One cannot get beyond the cloud in answering the "hows and whys," but the cloud was a reminder of the glory of God's eternal presence—like the Shekinah glory which filled the Temple of God. It's enough to know that where God is, Christ is there also! God was at work on mankind's behalf "when he raised him [Jesus] from the dead and seated him at his right hand in the heavenly realms, far above all rule and authority, power and dominion, and every title that can be given, not only in the present age but also in the one to come. And God placed all things under his feet and appointed him to be head over everything for the church, which is his body, the fulness of him who fills everything in every way" (Eph. 1:20-23).

The Ascension is an introduction to Jesus' ministry of intercession. As Barclay noted:

> It is the consistent belief of the New Testament that Jesus ascended to make intercession for us. It is Christ who is at the right hand of God who indeed intercedes for us (Rom. 8:34). He always lives to make

2. *Ibid.*

intercession for us (Heb. 7:25). He appears in the presence of God on our behalf (Heb. 9:24). In Him we have an Advocate in the presence of God (1 John 2:1). He is the Mediator who stands between man and God to bring man and God together, and He continues that mediating work in the presence of God (Heb. 8:6; 12:24; 1 Tim. 2:1, 5). Jesus ascended, not to end His work for men, but to continue His work for men that . . . He may still carry on His ministry of intercession and mediation for men.[3]

When a person faces something that hits him like a jolt, Jesus is at the right hand of God pleading for him. While one is asleep, Jesus is still on the job reminding God of his needs. When temptation seems to drain a man's resistance, Jesus is wide-awake to give him the strength to win. When that awful sense of guilt hangs over a fellow dragging his infirmities before him and dredging up past failures and sins, Jesus is his Advocate at the very throne of heaven! Jesus said, "It is for your good that I am going away" (John 16:7).

Most are familiar with the fact that the Holy Spirit, the Comforter, could not come until Jesus went away. Nor could Jesus' ministry of intercession be unlimited. But sometimes "there is an unrecognized good in the going. A parent takes a small boy to camp and goes home without him. . . . But his going was for the child's good; the child must learn how to live with his contemporaries, how to carry his own load, how to play and how to get along without the constant oversight of his parents. There are times when (it seems) God disappears to put us on our own. He wants persons, not puppets."[4]

The Bible gives a word of encouragement: "Since we

---

3. *Ibid.*, p. 320.
4. George Arthur Buttrick, ed., *The Interpreter's Bible,* Vol. 9 (New York: Abingdon Press, 1954), p. 29.

have a great High Priest who has gone into heaven, Jesus the Son of God, let us hold firmly to the faith we profess. For we do not have a High Priest who is unable to sympathize with our weaknesses, but we have one who has been tempted in every way, just as we are—yet was without sin. Let us then approach the throne of grace with confidence, so that we may receive mercy and find grace to help us in our time of need" (Heb. 4:14-16).

The Ascension of Jesus is an introduction to His availability! Arnold Airhart points out that during the 40 days following the Resurrection the disciples "had already learned that 'out of sight' did not mean out of reach. They would be assured of His nearness."[5]

Jesus is at home in our times, and those who love Him and try to serve Him think of Him as being near and close at hand. He belongs not just to the first century but to all time and eternity. He is at home in a great teeming city, in the crowded apartments of the poor, and in the mansions of the rich. He sits by the scholar in his study, and is by the side of the laborer in the street. Still He welcomes little children, and they love Him. He is our contemporary, as modern as our latest breath!

William Barclay states it emphatically: "The Ascension gave the disciples the certainty that they had a Friend, not only on earth, but in heaven. . . . To die is not to go out into the dark; it is to go to Him."[6]

A. T. Robertson adds: "Now that the Ascension has come they are no longer in despair. Joy becomes the note of victory as it is today. No other note can win victories for Christ. The bells rang in heaven to greet the return of

---

5. Arnold E. Airhart, *Beacon Bible Expositions,* Vol. 5 (Kansas City: Beacon Hill Press of Kansas City, 1977), pp. 22-23.

6. William Barclay, "The Gospel of Luke," *The Daily Study Bible* (Philadelphia: The Westminster Press, 1953), p. 314.

Jesus there, but He set the carillon of joy to ringing on earth in human hearts in all lands and for all time."[7]

The Ascension of Jesus Is an Anticipation

The Ascension is an anticipation of hope and heaven. The Son of Man was taken bodily up into heaven. He told His followers: "Because I live, you also will live" (John 14:19). His going is a reminder that someday we, too, shall be taken up into heaven. What a great hope for tomorrow! The Good News depends upon it. It's illogical to tell men they must do God's will and accept His gospel of grace if one's obligation has no eternal significance; that nothing ultimately depends on it!

Years ago a small town in Maine was proposed for the site of a great hydro-electric plant. Since a dam would be built across the river, the town would be submerged. When the project was announced, the people were given many months to arrange their affairs and to relocate.

During the time before the dam was built, an interesting thing happened. All improvements ceased! No painting was done. No repairs were made on the buildings and roads and sidewalks. Day by day the whole town got shabbier and shabbier. A long time before the dam was built and the waters came, the town looked uncared for and abandoned—even though the people had not yet moved away. One citizen explained: "Where there is no faith in the future, there is no power in the present." That town was cursed with hopelessness!

Jesus' ascension is the proof that we are destined for heaven, not for the grave. We are destined for glory, not for annihilation! The hymn writer put it well:

---

7. Archibald Thomas Robertson, *Word Pictures in the New Testament,* vol. 2 (Nashville: Broadman Press, 1930), p. 298.

Changed from glory into glory,
Till in heav'n we take our place,
Till we cast our crowns before Thee,
Lost in wonder, love, and praise.

—CHARLES WESLEY

The ascension of Jesus is an anticipation of His return! His people are looking forward with eager expectation to the great day when the Ascended One will come back again on the clouds of heaven. Those two messengers announced: "This same Jesus, who has been taken from you into heaven, will come back in the same way you have seen him go into heaven" (Acts 1:11).

When Jesus came as a baby on that pallet of straw, all the predictions of His first advent were fulfilled. Just as assuredly, all the predictions of His second coming shall be literally fulfilled. It is unmistakably taught in the Bible. Only the subject of the Atonement gets more space than the return of Jesus Christ. In the New Testament the second coming of Jesus is mentioned 318 times. For every time the first coming is mentioned, the second coming of Christ is mentioned 8 times! Whole chapters such as Matthew 24, Luke 21, and Mark 13 are given to teach the second coming of Christ. Whole books are built on the theme of Jesus' promised return: 1 and 2 Thessalonians!

Robert G. Lee has written, "Many churches today consider it [the Second Coming] *incidental.* The churches of the first century considered it *fundamental.* They were certain about the certainty of it."[8]

Many writers try to explain away the meaning of the second coming of Jesus. Jesus' return is more than just the spiritual presence of Christ in each believer. The return of Christ is more than the promised coming of the Holy Spirit

---

8. Robert G. Lee, *Great Is the Lord* (Westwood, New Jersey: Fleming H. Revell Company, 1955), p. 133.

34

at Pentecost or to believers at any age. The promise of Jesus' return is not to be equated with the death of a Christian. It is the visible, bodily, glorious reappearing of our Lord Jesus Christ. The Bible says: "Look, he is coming with the clouds, and every eye will see him" (Rev. 1:7). I don't understand all that it means, but I believe it will happen just as the Bible says! In fact, Jesus' return is the next great event in the life and ministry of the Son of God!

The ascension of Jesus is an anticipation of His ultimate victory. Paul describes Christ's return vividly: "For the Lord himself will come down from heaven, with a loud command, with the voice of the archangel and with the trumpet call of God, and the dead in Christ will rise first. After that, we who are still alive and are left will be caught up with them in the clouds to meet the Lord in the air. And so we will be with the Lord forever. Therefore encourage each other with these words" (1 Thess. 4:16-18).

> *Lo! He comes, with clouds descending,*
> *Once for favoured sinners slain;*
> *Thousand thousand saints attending*
> *Swell the triumph of His train;*
> *Allelujah! Allelujah!*
> *God appears on earth to reign!*
> —JOHN CENNICK

Winston Churchill became prime minister of the British Empire in 1940 when Britain was reeling on the brink of defeat. Churchill cried out: "You ask, What is our aim? I can answer in one word: Victory—victory at all costs, victory in spite of all terror, victory, however long and hard the road may be."

Jesus is coming to reign in victory. He is going to keep His promise: "I shall return!"

Like you, I have never seen Jesus with these eyes. Only with the eyes of faith have I known He is right here all along. While I have not always been faithful, He has been. I want Jesus to come in person so I can see Him and tell Him I love Him. I'm looking forward to His return!

One feels like the little boy whose father found him awake late in the night. The boy was chuckling out loud and saying: "If you only knew what I know! If only you knew what I know!"

The father discovered his boy was reading a wild west thriller. He had gotten into the middle of the book and the plot was getting thicker and more suspenseful. The hero was being wronged and abused and disgraced. The villain seemed to be winning and gloating in his triumph. The lad couldn't stand it any longer and turned to the last page to see how the story was going to come out. There he saw the hero gloriously vindicated and the villain punished.

Going back to the middle of the story, instead of agonizing, he was rejoicing in the midst of the dark plot. He knew that all would end well and he laughed out loud: "If you only knew what I know!"

Happlily, I have read clear through God's Book. The pressures and frustrations of life may come, sorrows and testings may be around the corner—I don't know all about tomorrow! Things may seem topsy-tervy! We may be left reeling from the blows of the unexpected! But I have read the last chapter: "I, Jesus, have sent my angel to give you this testimony for the churches. . . . Yes, I am coming soon!" (Rev. 22:16, 20).

If you only knew what I know! "In all these things we are more than conquerors through him who loved us" (Rom. 8:37).

Why a treatise on the Ascension? How do we answer the question, "So what?" Let me illustrate.

Churchill was invited to speak at Harrow, the school where he had attended as a boy. The headmaster told the students: "Bring your notebooks and copy down everything he says. You are going to hear the greatest living Englishman."

Well along in years, Churchill stood on the school platform and put his fingers in his vest-pockets, pulled his glasses down on his nose, and looked over them at the student audience. No doubt, as he stood there, he could remember the shy, skinny boy named Winston Churchill, who stuttered—but who became the greatest master of English speech in modern history. Looking at those bright boys, he realized that life could bring them plenty of hard knocks. So Churchill made his speech.

He said: "Never give up! Never give up! Never, never, never!" And then sat down.

In the light of Jesus' promise to return, the challenge comes: "Never give up! Never, never, never!" Jesus is coming again! He shall return!

CHAPTER 3

What to Do Next?

Acts 1:12-26

While in Minneapolis, Fletcher Tink and his family had seen several Easter pageants during Holy Week. Leaving the city en route to be missionaries in Bolivia, the three-year-old daughter, Kayla, said wistfully: "We're sure going to miss Jesus, aren't we?"

The disciples' mood after the ascension of Jesus is one of foot-shuffling and thumb-twiddling. It seems they are standing around in the corridors waiting for something to happen—like during an intermission between acts of a play! There seems to be a pensive mood: "We're sure going to miss Jesus, aren't we?"

William P. Barker put it well:

> If the last mighty act of God had been the resurrection and ascension, today there would be no church. If the pattern outlined in the first chapter of Acts had continued, the apostles and others would never have left Jerusalem to witness. They would have formed a religious club, perhaps a "Jesus Memorial Society." Like other such groups, it would probably have had meetings, dues, minutes, and the usual club perapher-

nalia. In spite of valiant endeavors by loyal adherents to "keep the organization going," the band of believers in the Risen Jesus Christ would eventually have dwindled away and in time the memory of Jesus would have become an interesting footnote in the history books of the Middle East.[1]

The disciples hike back from the Mount of Olives, a little less than a mile, to their Upper Room headquarters in Jerusalem. Things seem rather at loose ends, disconnected, directionless! In fact, these verses are a potpourri of incidentals! In the lull, Peter can't stand the awkward silences. In the absence of Jesus, he takes his place as the leader of the group. Though he had denied his Master those three indelible times, Peter had been forgiven and restored to his responsibility as the shepherd to Jesus' flock. With his characteristic impetuous action, Peter tries to get things started again.

Peter takes note that the 11 remaining apostles are all present in the room. The absence of the defector seems like a big gap in Jesus' original plan for 12 apostles—symbolic of the 12 tribes of Israel, the formation of the new Israel. Isn't it strange how the absent member looms larger than the faithful ones who are standing by? Peter concludes that the answer to the problem of the lull is an organizational arrangement. Coming down from the glorious moment of Jesus' ascension, they are suddenly into a administrative problem. But, then, life is a strange mixture of rapture and routine, of scaling the heights and digging in the valleys. We can't have one without the other!

Having found oneself down out of the clouds of glory, one wonders, "Where's the excitement, the miracles, the exuberance I used to have?" Having come from the pinnacles of spiritual blessing, one discovers the grimy nuts

---

1. William P. Barker, *They Stood Boldly* (Westwood, N.J.: Fleming H. Revell Company, 1967.), pp. 19-20.

and bolts of the workaday world. Perhaps one thinks something is wrong. Satan would accuse a person of losing out spiritually—but, of course, that's his job! What should one do next?

There are lessons to be learned from the mistakes of others. One can observe Peter and the disciples in a similar situation—and they are very human, just like the rest of us.

There Seems to Be a Desire to Do Something to Fill the Vacancy They Felt

That gnawing sense of a broken fellowship from their original circle begins to dominate their thinking. So Peter, in his characteristic way, gives in to the urge to "do something." Months before, in the splendor of the Mount of Transfiguration, Peter was awed by the miraculous appearance of Elijah and Moses surrouding Jesus. He was enraptured—but didn't know how to respond to it. The Bible literally describes him: "Peter, having nothing to say, said, 'Let's build three tents—one for Jesus, one for Elijah, one for Moses!'" One wonders why Peter thought Elijah and Moses would need a tent!

In these uncertain days after Jesus' ascension, Peter is sure the solution is to "do something!" He makes a hasty assessment of the whole situation and decides to administrate an election. Surely God expects us to do something—doesn't He?

The young, growing Christian can come to a time in his spiritual life when he asks sincerely, "What else is there? Is this all? Isn't there something more? I must not have done something right!" That kind of vagueness is not God's way of directing His children. There's an ebb and flow of the spiritual tide because our humanity has to

40

catch up with our new life in Christ; with new values and new desires!

One man has testified:

> Gnawing within me for years, unspoken, lurked the fear that if I completely gave myself to God, I'd wind up: (1) either waving a big, floppy Bible preaching somewhere on a street corner, or (2) going as a missionary to the scariest part of Africa. I couldn't think of two worse fates: floppy Bibles are for home reading, and please, dear Lord, I'm not even a big-game hunter . . . not Africa! Then I told Him I was willing. Now I know better. I was doubting God's love. Suppose God did want me in Africa. How would He let me know? He'd make me *want* to go! I'd want to go to Africa so bad you couldn't keep me in the United States.
>
> God works through your will. The further I go with Jesus Christ the more confidence I have in what I want to do. Every day I keep continually committing my will to Christ. Believing in Him, I believe He works through my will. The will of God is not some thing you *do;* it is something you *are.*[2]

It is a mistake to think "much doing" is the answer of the soul. A fanatic is defined as one who, having lost sight of the goal, doubles his efforts! It is much more dignified to say, "We are moving in cycles," rather than "running around in circles."

There Seems to Be a Desire to Keep Things as They Were

Whatever organization did exist among the apostles was interrupted when Jesus returned to heaven. Peter was sure they must hang onto the past forms. He was convinced they must maintain the status quo. The arrange-

---

2. Howard Butt, *The Velvet-Covered Brick* (New York: Harper and Row, Publishers, 1973), p. 116.

ment of 12 apostles must be kept intact—or so Peter decided! Good organization by itself can never create a happy and prosperous home, nation, or church. Organization can become a straitjacket which paralyzes the Spirit of Christ. Of course, the Spirit without any frame of reference is like the wind with no sails to catch it for making forward progress.

Robert Townsend, in his book *Up the Organization,* reminds us that it's about 11 times easier to start something than it is to stop it. The British created a civil service job in 1803 calling for a man to stand on the Cliffs of Dover with a spyglass. He was instructed to ring a bell if he saw Napoleon coming. The job was finally abolished in 1945.

What Peter did not understand is that God apparently didn't care to keep things just as they were. He had a whole new plan—one that reached far beyond filling the post of a discarded apostleship. His plan for the future was beyond their small dreams. It was more than 12 men could handle!

Something is not bad just because it is old, nor is it good just because it is new. By the same token, the church should be more concerned about where it is going than where it has been!

Peter, hanging onto the old form, reminds one of an incident Olan Hendrix tells in his book *Management and the Christian Worker:* "There was a British military team trying to cut down on the manpower used in handling a field cannon. Always there had been six men assigned to each cannon, but there were only five jobs. The men studied each job and went to the instruction manual. From the first edition on, every manual called for a crew of six. Finally they located the man who had written the manual originally, a retired general, and they asked him what the sixth man was supposed to do. He replied, 'The sixth man? He holds the horses.' They had not used horses for many,

many years, but the job persisted. No reason was necessary; precedent was reason enough!"[3]

Peter misunderstood what made the past great. It was not having 12 apostles; it was having Jesus in their midst! In the lulls of life, when tempted to look back to what seems a better day, be sure to get a grasp on what really makes the difference. It is a continuing relationship with Jesus! Hang onto that! Remember, too, that He is with us in the valleys of life just as assuredly He is on the mountaintop where the glory of God shines bright!

There Seems to Be a Desire
to Want God to Approve Our Plans

Peter led the 120 disciples to establish two basic qualifications for the apostleship candidates. Two men were the finalists, having met the qualifications. The Bible says, "Then they prayed, 'Lord, you know everyone's heart. Show us which of these two you have chosen to take over this apostolic ministry, which Judas left to go where he belongs'" (Acts 1:24-25).

Those 120 people were sincere; they prayed earnestly; they were eager to do the right things—but basically, they wanted God to approve *their* plan to fill the vacancy left by Judas.

How many times have we gone to God, handed Him our set of life-plans, and anxiously awaited His approval. Approval on *our* terms—not His! "Here, Lord," we say, "I'm going to do this and this! Please put your stamp of approval on my plans. Sign it here, no—not there! Right here!"

---

3. Roy E. Carnahan, *Creative Pastoral Management* (Kansas City: Beacon Hill Press of Kansas City, 1976), p. 66.

When the Israelites came through the desert to Kadesh-Barnea, God wanted them to proceed right on into the Promised Land. He would have guaranteed them victory. But those elders sent in spies to check out the land. They asked the wrong questions. Listening to the majority report of the spies, the Israelites asked, "Are our opponents too big for us?" They should have been asking, "Is any thing too hard for the Lord?" (Gen. 18:14, KJV).

The leaders ended up debating, "Shall we retreat this way or that way?" God was expected to put His "OK" on their failure!

First, one must understand "why we are doing this" before he can begin to understand "what we are doing." Only then can one understand "how we will do it!"

Peter made a hasty assessment which led him to misunderstand the problem. That's why he came to a wrong conclusion. It probably didn't make any difference to God which man was selected—both were qualified. One was chosen, but neither is mentioned again in Scripture. These good men faded from view in the biblical record. They remind one of the inscription on the state of Virginia's monument to the Confederate Unknown Soldiers: "Who they were none knows—what they were all know!"

It is strange that the disciples prayed for God's guidance, but then selected Matthias by chance, not choice. The Bible says, "They drew lots, and the lot fell to Matthias; so he was added to the eleven apostles" (Acts 1: 26). The usual method of casting lots was to put stones with names written on them into a vessel which was shaken until one name fell out—a matter of chance. It is significant that the disciples never again used lots for making decisions after Pentecost, the coming of the indwelling Holy Spirit.

One must seek God's plan—not His approval on one's own plan!

I asked for grace to lift me high
　Above the world's depressing cares;
God sent me sorrows—with a sigh
　I said, "He has not heard my prayers."

I asked for light, that I might see
　My path along life's thorny road;
But clouds and darkness shadowed me
　When I expected light from God.

I asked for peace, that I might rest
　To think my sacred duties o'er,
When, lo! such horrors filled my breast
　As I had never felt before.

"And, oh," I cried, "can this be prayer
　Whose plaints the steadfast mountains move?
Can this be Heaven's prevailing care?
　And, O my God, is this Thy love?"

But soon I found that sorrow, worn
　As Duty's garment, strength supplies,
And out of darkness meekly borne
　Unto the righteousness light doth rise.

And soon I found that fears which stirred
　My startled soul God's will to do,
On me more lasting peace conferred
　Than in life's calm I ever knew.

—Author Unknown

The question must be asked: "Do I want God's plan—
or God's approval on my plans?" Jayne Garrison relates
this beautiful story:

　It was not long after I became acquainted with Olie
　that I learned how fervently he wished to become a
　physician. To me his desire was more than justified, for

45

he was intelligent, friendly, enthusiastic, compassionate and gentle—perfect traits for a man of medicine. But then, I loved him—so much in fact that I left college, married him and then sat back waiting for his acceptance to medical school.

But the letter of acceptance never came. After several months of disappointment, we both realized that Olie was not going to get into medical school. It was the deepest heartache either of us had experienced and the most difficult part of it was finding a reason for his rejection. His grades were high, his desire strong, his mind was willing to meet the strain of study, and I was ready to face the financial struggle.

Being Christians, we had naturally prayed for his acceptance. Surely God could use a good Christian doctor, I reasoned, and I prayed earnestly, begging God to help Olie get into medical school if it were His will. When it appeared that my prayers had gone unanswered, I shrugged Olie's rejection off with the old statement, "It's not what you know but who you know that counts." Faced with empty plans for the future, Olie and I left our home in Texas and journeyed to Minnesota, where Olie was to do graduate work in biochemistry. But there was so much Olie did not know that several times during the first year he longed to quit graduate school entirely. I encouraged him to reapply to medical school, and again I prayed that he might be accepted. And again he was rejected. The day that we received the last rejection letter, I cried bitterly to God. "Why, God? Why can't You let Olie do something he loves? Don't You know I don't want to be a poor scientist's wife?"

And there it was! The problem was suddenly very clear to me. I had never really been praying for Olie—only for myself. Being the daughter of a minister, I saw the medical world as guaranteed freedom from past financial burdens. It was a life that I had wanted for Olie because it would be good for me. The realization of my selfishness made me feel wretched. When I prayed again, it was simply to ask God to help Olie and me find a purpose to our lives. It was a prayer that I kept repeating.

46

With that, things did not get easier—only better. Olie's first scientific triumph came later in the form of a publication concerning the purification of a protein that may someday benefit emphysema patients.

"Olie," I said to him the day we learned that his research was to be published, "if you still want to be a doctor, I'll bet you could get into medical school now."

Olie smiled. "I want to do research," he said. "I see that now."

I felt like crying. How could I have put so little faith in God? Here was a man who had been given the gift of discovery and at one time I had hoped he would not use it. I still claim that it is not what you know but Who you know that counts. Thank goodness the One we know is God.[4]

In times of the spiritual lull, we need to open up our lives and let God fill in the blanks. The Bible says, "Delight thyself also in the Lord; and he shall give thee the desires of thine heart. Commit thy way unto the Lord; trust also in him; and he shall bring it to pass"(Ps. 37:4-5, KJV). "Wait on the Lord: be of good courage, and he shall strengthen thine heart: wait, I say, on the Lord" (Ps. 27:14, KJV). God just wants His child to be open to Him in a surrender without bitterness, a surrender of love!

Some folk strain at the idea of submitting to God, of giving in to Him only because they feel forced to. They're like the old Scottish elder who opposed the merger between the Scottish Presbyterian Church with the Church of Scotland. When the union took place, he gave in because he believed the will of the church expressed the will of God. But he muttered aloud, "It's all wrong, I tell you. It's all wrong—but evidently it's the will of God!"

The Bible says: "For God is at work within you, helping you want to obey Him, and then helping you do what

4. Jayne Garrison, "Be Careful What You Ask For," *Guideposts*, January, 1976.

He wants" (Phil. 2:13, TLB). It is love opening up to whatever God designs!

This is a way of life—through the mountaintops and through the valleys. It isn't just an emergency measure of the moment. The surrendered life isn't always emotionally rewarding: "It is not always a matter of following a star; sometimes it is no more than the footprints left in the dust."[5]

One fellow commented, "I have known young Christians to be disturbed by the testimonies of good and well-meaning people who gave the impression they were always blest. Such claims challenge a new convert to seek for perpetual bliss, too; and after a fruitless search, he may be tempted to give up altogether. Seasoned saints help new converts when they honestly confess to the ebb as well as the flow of spiritual tides." Jesus put it plainly: "If any man will come after me, let him deny himself, and take up his cross, and follow me" (Matt. 16:24, KJV). God's will and our high emotions are not always synonymous.

Though Peter and the disciples were in the lull, they did remain safe spiritually because they stayed in the circle of obedience. Jesus had instructed them to stay in Jerusalem and wait for the Holy Spirit's coming. Continuing steadfastly in prayer, they stuck with it until the answer came! There was a gritty determination in their prayers. The Greek word describing their prayers is used also of an army attacking a walled citadel, hammering at the gates with desperation to win! One must not overlook the fact they stayed together in obedience to Jesus!

If a person is in the wrong place, the right place is empty! Happy is the man who knows he is in God's place at God's time, doing his best to serve, and leaving the results with the Lord!

---

5. Buttrick, *Interpreter's Bible,* 9:33. ·

CHAPTER 4

The Unveiling of the Spirit

Acts 2:1-13

In describing the concept of the Trinity, it has been said that the Father is God in creation; the Son is God in history; the Holy Spirit is God in the present tense!

The story of Pentecost becomes the occasion for the unveiling of God in the present tense—in the person of the Holy Spirit. He did not come into existence at Pentecost, but He was unveiled that day, coming to occupy men's lives.

Pentecost literally means "fiftieth" and became known as "The Feast of Weeks." Technically, it is the first day after seven weeks, or 49 days, after the Feast of Passover. The Passover festival is the annual celebration of the exodus of the Jews from Egypt's slavery. It is the great Day of Atonement and Deliverance. On the 50th day following Passover, the Jews celebrate Pentecost which commemorates the giving of the Mosaic Law from God at Mount Sinai. Also, Pentecost is a festival for thanksgiving to God for the first harvests of the year. Being in late spring, it was the best time for first century Jews to travel in the Mediterranean world. Thousands of pilgrims came annually for the Pentecost celebration, the favorite holiday of the Jews at that time.

Jesus had been crucified during the Passover Feast —His was the greatest act of Atonement and Deliverance! On the Cross, Jesus was the Paschal Lamb of God who took away our sins. Of course, the Resurrection came on the third day, and the Risen Christ walked among His disciples for 40 days. On the Mount of Olives, Jesus ascended into heaven on a great cloud, and His men returned to Jerusalem in obedience to the Master, waiting for the promise of the Comforter.

On the morning of the Day of Pentecost, 120 disciples of Jesus were together celebrating the holiday. God's timing was ripe—and right! Dramatically, the Holy Spirit was unveiled to the followers of Jesus. A great power was unleashed into the hearts of men! The promise Jesus had made was fulfilled: "Wait for the gift my Father promised . . . in a few days you will be baptized with the Holy Spirit. . . . But you will receive power when the Holy Spirit comes on you; and you will be my witnesses in Jerusalem, and in all Judea and Samaria, and to the ends of the earth" (Acts 1:4-8). In that God-given dynamic, the Early Church was launched on its mission to make disciples in the power of the Spirit!

Centuries later, when men were making creeds to systematize Christian doctrine, they could only say: "I believe in the Holy Spirit." Religious debaters had taken away the experience of the indwelling Spirit and replaced it with a belief or creedal statement. One major newspaper commented, "There are few doctrines more perplexing to the average man than the doctrine of the Holy Spirit." But to the Early Church, the Holy Spirit was no puzzle. He was a dynamic power and presence, the heartbeat of their faith! Without the Spirit of God controlling within, religion is simply a demand without a dynamic!

Dr. E. Stanley Jones wrote: "I read a book entitled *Come, Holy Spirit, Come,* and the only reference in the book to the Holy Spirit was at the end of one sermon: 'Come, Holy Spirit, come and dwell with us.' That was all. It was a title and not a teaching, a label and not a life. . . . it was moonlight instead of sunlight."[6]

Pentecost was the day God turned on the power switch and unveiled the Holy Spirit!

Pentecost Announced the Supremacy of the Spirit

With Jesus ascended and seated at the right hand of God the Father, a new era was launched: "When the day of Pentecost came, they were all together in one place. Suddenly a sound like the blowing of a violent wind came from heaven and filled the whole house where they were sitting. They saw what seemed to be tongues of fire that separated and came to rest on each of them. All of them were filled with the Holy Spirit and began to speak in other tongues [margin, "languages"] as the Spirit enabled them" (Acts 2:1-4).

On the day which Pentecost commemorated, the giving of the Law from Mount Sinai, lightning and thunder shook the mountain as the dramatic presence of God ushered in a new era. And now, on this Pentecost Day, miracles surrounded the opening of another epoch in God's economy. The sound of wind, the fiery tongues, the miracle of communication all combined to announce the dispensation of the Holy Spirit. G. Campbell Morgan, preacher and Bible scholar, wrote: "We must remember that these signs were initial; they were incomplete. They produced no final result. They were necessary to arrest the attention of Jeru-

---

6. E. Stanley Jones, *The Way to Power and Poise* (New York: Abingdon-Cokesbury Press, 1949), p. 28.

salem. . . . They were Divine, direct and positive, but they were transient, never repeated because never needed."

These miraculous manifestations were signs or symbols of the supremacy of the Holy Spirit. It is profitable to look at each one.

First, there is the "sound like the blowing of a violent wind." This is the symbol of power! One cannot see the wind, but one can see its effects—mighty, powerful, irresistible! The sound of wind filled the house.

There is a certain mystery about wind. In Jesus' conversation with Nicodemus illustrating the Spirit, He said: "The wind blows wherever it pleases. You may hear its sound, but you cannot tell where it comes from or where it is going" (John 3:8).

Wind also has the elements necessary for life. The English word *spirit* comes from the Latin word *spiritus,* meaning "breath." The Greek word for "spirit," *pneuma,* also means "wind" or "breath." It was Job who said, "The spirit of God hath made me, and the breath of the Almighty hath given me life" (Job 33:4, KJV). The Holy Spirit is the breath of God! God made man and the Bible says, "The Lord God formed man of the dust of the ground, and breathed into his nostrils the breath of life; and man became a living soul" (Gen. 2:7, KJV). The sound of the wind was symbolic of God's breath of life given to man. God was at work re-creating man for His kingdom.

> *Breathe on me, Breath of God,*
> *Fill me with life anew.*
> —EDWIN HATCH

Wind can bring a refreshing atmosphere. Many a day we have wished for a breeze to clear the air and refresh our spirits. The Holy Spirit wishes to sweep among us, bringing heaven's atmosphere of joy and peace, blowing away the stale, polluted air of selfishness and sin.

Wind has freedom. It is free to move without hindrance. The Holy Spirit cannot be regulated or legislated; there must be freedom of the Spirit.

Second, there are "what seemed to be tongues of fire that separated and came to rest on each of them" (Acts 2:3). The fire is the symbol of purity! Apparently the fire looked like lightning dividing and setting on each of them. The experience of cleansing was for each individual—not just for the group as a whole. The flame rested on them—a visual reminder of God's imparted power and purity.

Back in the Old Testament a pillar of fire guarded the Israelites at night and guided them by day. That fiery cloud entered the tabernacles' holy of holies, and the altar fires were sustained by a mysterious flame. It represented the Spirit of God among His people. However, the Spirit of God departed from the disobedient nation and the glory of God departed from among them. The tabernacle gave way to the Temple, and temple worship was filled with formality—the Spirit was long gone!

The Holy Spirit came on the Day of Pentecost to temples not made by hands. He entered God's people to make them pure and holy for God's use. He came to cleanse the hearts of those awaiting disciples.

During the contest of faith between Elijah and the 850 false prophets of Baal, the real and living God answered by fire. A sacrificial animal was placed on the altar of Baal. His henchmen chanted and danced and screamed until late afternoon—but no fire came. Elijah, grinning at the exhaustion of Baal's prophets, soaked his sacrificial animal with water and prayed a short prayer—just equivalent to 53 English words. God answered by fire from heaven. It consumed the water, the sacrifical animal, and even the rocks of the altar. He, the living God, answered the prayers of His people on that Day of Pentecost. He stood the test then, and He will stand the test of faith today!

Fire purifies, cleanses, and refines. Fire purges the dross of impurites and sludge from gold and silver. Who shall stand in God's holy place? "He that hath clean hands, and a pure heart" (Ps. 24:4, KJV).

When Isaiah had a vision of the Lord, he cried out: "Woe is me! for I am undone; because I am a man of unclean lips" (Isa. 6:5, KJV).

Then a seraph took a live coal from the altar and touched Isaiah's lips, saying: "Thine iniquity is taken away, and thy sin purged" (Isa. 6:8, KJV).

On Pentecost, the fire of God's Spirit came to rest on men to cleanse their hearts from the sin nature!

Milo Arnold tells of a U.S. Marine who had been surrounded by the enemy in the Korean War. For 30 days of horror, the marine didn't dare be off guard; he never removed his shoes or clothing. He slept in a foxhole. During that time the marine neither shaved nor washed. Not once did he have hot food. From crawling in mud and filth like an animal, his clothing was rotting off his body. He faced death without relief.

Finally, freed from the enemy trap, the young man was taken to a hospital. Medical aides cut the rags and muck from his body. Then came the happiest moment of all, he was put into a warm tub of soapy water. Stretching out, the marine luxuriated in his first bath for a month. After a shave and a haircut, he crawled between clean sheets and enjoyed a hot meal served in bed. His comment was, "If I live to be a hundred years of age, I'll never forget how good that bath felt."

Arnold added,

> Yes, to be clean; to be freed from the clinging, contaminating things, is an adventure.
> The disciples found it. They had been stained with pride and self-centeredness. They had been given to the sin of greed and jealousy. But at Pentecost some-

thing happened. They found a deep, inner cleansing. The Holy Spirit not only came to them in the presence signified by the rushing, mighty wind, but also in the cleansing signified by the purging tongues of flame. They were made persons fit for the indwelling Presence. They were to feel for the first time the uncontaminated life freed from self and sin. Now they were made fit for the presence of the Holy Spirit. The blood of Jesus Christ had cleansed them from *all* sin.[7]

Third, they "began to speak in other tongues [margin, "languages"] as the Spirit enabled them" (Acts 2:4). This is the symbol of proclamation!

These Spirit-filled men began to praise God and witness to the mighty acts of God—probably in their Galilean accents, but people rushing in to hear what was going on heard them in their own languages. It was a miracle of tellling and a miracle of hearing. Miraculous communication was necessary because spectators had gathered from at least 17 nations. Each spectator heard the message of God in his own dialect or language, so there could be no doubt about what the message was! There was no "unknown" tongue here: "Each one heard them speaking in his own language" (Acts 2:6); "How is it that each of us hears them in his own native language?" (Acts 2:8); "We hear them declaring the wonders of God in our own tongues!" (Acts 2:11). Such spontaneous, miraculous proclamation was symbolic of "new methods of conquest: the preaching of the Word, anointed by the Spirit, in the dialects of the people. The kingdom would be extended throughout the world by word of mouth and by word of pen. The Church was launched on a speaking mission."[8]

---

7. Milo L. Arnold, *The Christian Adventure* (Kansas City: Beacon Hill Press of Kansas City, 1974), p. 64.

8. W. T. Purkiser, Richard S. Taylor, and Willard H. Taylor, *God, Man, and Salvation* (Kansas City: Beacon Hill Press of Kansas City, 1977), pp. 490-91.

In the Old Testament, after the Flood, rebellious men decided to build the great Tower of Babel as an act of defiance. God confused their tongues into different languages and the project came to a halt because the men were unable to be one. Pentecost became a reversal of Babel. At Babel men were confounded because one language became many. At Pentecost, they were confounded because many languages became one.

Pentecost Introduced the Occupancy of the Spirit

The three signs—wind, fire, and languages—were miracles alright, but the supreme miracle of Pentecost was the coming of the Holy Spirit to occupy and reside in men. Charles Higgins, writing in the *Herald of Holiness,* states: "All of them were filled with the Holy Spirit (Acts 2:4). The Spirit of God rushed into their lives as One eager to possess the building designed to be His home. As soon as the door was open—He was in! So quickly—so easily—so effortlessly!"

When the Holy Spirit filled them, He took possession of them. The Spirit controls the man whom He fills, occupying the center of a man's life where there are no hindrances or barriers.

The Bible gives a progressive revelation: "Christmas speaks of God *with* us; Good Friday, Easter, and the Ascension speak of God *for* us; while Pentecost speaks of God *in* us."[9] Pentecost is the climax of the other events! Without Pentecost, the Cross would have become ineffective. It would be like building a beautiful automobile, but neglecting to put in a motor for power.

God looks for a place of occupancy. First, God dwelt in a holy temple; then God dwelt in a Holy Person—Jesus

---

9. *Ibid.,* p. 484.

Christ. But now, God dwells in a holy people—those who accept the gift of the Spirit.

God in the Old Testament is Light; God in Jesus is Life; God in us is Power! The Holy Spirit has come to occupy our hearts.

A missionary from Japan had gone home to England during his furlough. Some members of the Japanese emperor's family were touring Europe and by previous arrangements came to visit the well-known missionary. After a fine visit, the royal family continued on their tour.

Later in the day some Japanese officials from the embassy also dropped in. One of them said to the missionary, "You have been entertaining royalty here today."

Rather surprised, the missionary asked, "What makes you think so?"

The ambassador replied, "There is a perfume manufactured in our country for the exclusive use of royalty. No one else is allowed to use it. Its fragrance is evidenced in this apartment. We know you have had royal visitors today!"

Since the Holy Spirit has come to reside in God's children, the fragrance of His presence should be evidenced in their lives wherever and whenever they go. When one is a child of God, he is called to be a child of the King and to be occupied by Royalty!

The hope of the Church is Spirit-filled men and women!

Pentecost Underscored the Adequacy of the Spirit

The Bible says, "All of them were filled with the Holy Spirit and began to speak . . . as the Spirit enabled them" (Acts 2:4).

Without the filling of the Spirit, we are most inadequate. When we cease to depend on the Holy Spirit we cease to be dependable!

John Wesley was obviously spiritually inadequate before his personal Pentecost. He did his religious work without effectiveness. He preached with uncertainty. Trying to be a missionary, he was actually a mission field himself. But look what God did through him after his heartwarming experience at Aldersgate when the Holy Spirit came to occupy his heart. He was adequate in the Spirit.

Beyond natural powers, one can have the Spirit's inner adequacy, His divine enforcement.

The Word doesn't record one convert between the Crucifixion and Pentecost. It appears that for two months nothing happened. However, once filled with the Spirit, Jesus' followers came out from behind closed doors. As Fletcher Spruce pointed out: "The Sermon on the Mount didn't do it. The miracles and parables didn't go it. The Lord's Supper didn't do it. The atonement at Calvary didn't do it. The Easter Resurrection didn't do it. The Great Commission didn't do it. What, then, would it take to get the Church out from behind closed doors? One thing, and only one: Pentecost! . . . The two months of spiritual drought turned into a spiritual deluge. The 'no conversions' between Calvary and Pentecost was turned into 3,000 converts the first day."[10]

The Spirit-filled disciples began telling the mighty works of God! And wherever the mighty acts of God are proclaimed, the Holy Spirit goes to work. He gives power to witness; and, happily, He supplies the missing words in our stammering efforts!

---

10. Fletcher Clarke Spruce, *When God Comes* (Kansas City: Beacon Hill Press, 1950), p. 67.

These Spirit-filled men had a sense of adequacy in the Spirit. They were enabled to handle life with a poise born of the Spirit of God. Hiding behind closed doors had lost its appeal now. They acted like victors instead of victims!

During the Reformation, Martin Luther had been threatened to be killed if his enemies could reach him. Luther's friends put him in a great fortress overlooking the Rhine River. No one could attack him there.

However, in the isolation and security of the castle, Luther began to ponder his situation. Though he was safe and sound, he began to get discouraged. Finally he wrote a note to his old friend Phillip Melanchthon: "Phillip, everything is lost! There is no hope!"

Then, as God would have it, Luther came out of his castle hiding place. He was released from his security and went right back into life with its threats and uncertainties. In the midst of danger, Luther wrote the Reformation hymn: "A mighty fortress is our God, a bulwark never failing!"

It was *in the battle* that Martin Luther discovered the power of God and the adequacy of the Spirit! It's when we're squeezed to the wall that the sweet nature of Jesus will ooze out and bless even those who persecute us. "Be filled with the Spirit" comes ringing from the Bible!

The Holy Spirit enables us to forgive each other when we could not do it in our own strength. We find His Spirit to be adequate to unite us.

A few years after World War II, two women came from Asia to visit American churches and to witness to the mighty acts of God. One was the first Japanese lady permitted to leave Japan after the war; the other woman was a doctor from the Philippines. Though they came separately, they met for the first time one morning in their hotel at breakfast. What a painful experience! When the Filipino doctor saw the Japanese lady, she thought of the atrocities

59

committed against her family, friends, and her hospital by the Japanese invaders. She could not bring herself to say a word to the Japanese woman.

The next morning, the doctor heard a knock at her door. When she opened it, she was surprised to see the Japanese lady. With her head bowed low, the Japanese Christian asked quietly, "Can you forgive me for what my people did to you and your people? Will you go to breakfast with me?"

Suddenly, they were in each other's arms, weeping unashamedly. Dropping to their knees, they were reconciled by the power of the Holy Spirit. After they washed their faces, they went together to breakfast.[11]

The Holy Spirit came upon them. He empowered them to do what they could not do themselves. Yes, He is our great Enabler! He is our adequate Source of power. He is God's great Gift to all surrendered believers!

11. Barker, *They Stood Boldly,* pp. 26-27.

CHAPTER 5

Pentecost—Founder's Day

Acts 2 :14-41

One Sunday each fall, First Church of the Nazarene in Los Angeles celebrates "Founder's Day." The most recent "Founder's Day" was unforgettable! Worshippers sang hymns of praise in three different languages. The congregation prayed as one, each in his own language. They represented 30 nations of the world.

Los Angeles First Church was born in an atmosphere of holy joy. There was so much exuberance and enthusiasm among the founders that the first tabernacle, made of rough-hewn boards, was known as "The Glory Barn." On that day the congregation marched through the streets of Los Angeles to its first permanent location while 10,000 spectators lined the way to see the parade. The presence of God thrilled the hearts of those early Nazarenes, while others stood around in amazement, wondering what it was all about!

Dr. Phineas F. Bresee, founder of the Church of the Nazarene, described the "Glory Barn":

It was the fire that burned within that gilded its boards with glory and made them shimmer and shine with the light of heaven. When the multitude is gathered and there are hundreds of one mind and heart, and the Holy Ghost descends in His plenitude and power, that place is garnished with a beauty and glory in comparison with which all the adornings of Solomon's temple would be barrenness. Every board shines with the jewelled beauty of the New Jerusalem. What are carved marble and over-laying of gold and trimmings of silver; what are arches and turrets and spires, in comparison with the beauty of the Lord and the glory of the Divine Presence?

On the Day of Pentecost, the promised Holy Spirit fell on the gathered Church! The disciples were filled with the Spirit and there was such excitement and exuberance that spectators from 17 nations and languages and dialects came to witness the Founding Day of the Church! Heaven came down and glory filled their hearts with a holy joy.

The spectators were so amazed and perplexed they asked, "What does this mean?" (Acts 2:12). Something good was going to happen!

Some, having never seen such joy and enthusiasm, concluded, "They have had too much wine" (Acts 2:13). Alcohol can give a fellow a false sense of well-being. Momentarily he may forget his troubles, have the courage to speak to strangers, and feel that the world is wonderful because he is the most important person in it. But, when the intoxicant wears off, if he has a spark of self-respect, he despises what has happened.

Peter heard the accusations and said, "These men are not drunk, as you suppose. It's only nine in the morning! No, this is what was spoken by the prophet Joel: '. . . I will pour out my Spirit on all people'" (Acts 2:15-17). According to their custom, Jews drank wine only with meat which was served at night. No, these disciples of Jesus were God-intoxicated—that's what the English word, "enthusiasm," means: "Spirit-intoxicated!" The believers were so filled with the life of God they had a tremendous feeling of well-being. Like a puppy jumping up and down over the sheer joy of being alive, these Spirit-filled men expressed the delight of their newfound inner power!

One of the great mysteries is how did such an exciting, enthusiastic, infectious faith in Jesus ever become so identified with the seeming gloom, frowns, boredom, and joylessness found in some Christians' lives!

Immediately, in the presence of disciples and visitors, Peter began to reiterate the meaning of that dramatic Pentecost event—that Church Founding Day. His message can be summarized in this illustration: When the brilliant light of the sun is focused through a lens, there is a focal point just beyond where common paper or wood will burst into flames. The Sun of Righteousness who is the Light of the World was focused at the Cross through the open tomb. Just beyond, Pentecost became the focal point where the hearts of common, ordinary men burst into flaming witnesses of God's love and power.

In the Foreword to his book *Letters to Young Churches,* J. B. Phillips writes:

> The great difference between present-day Christianity and that of which we read . . . is that to us it is primarily a performance, to them it was a real experience. We are apt to reduce the Christian religion to a code, or at best a rule of heart and life. To these men it is quite plainly the invasion of their lives by a new quality of life altogether. They do not hesitate to describe this as Christ "living in" them. . . . These early Christians were on fire with the conviction that they had become, through Christ, literally sons of God; they were pioneers of a new humanity, founders of a new Kingdom. They still speak to us across the centuries. Perhaps if we believed what they believed, we might achieve what they achieved.[1]

1. J. B. Phillips, *Letters to Young Churches* (New York: The Macmillan Company, 1956), p. xiv.

Pentecost Makes an Appeal to the Mind—
It Explains God's Truth

When a professor at Nazarene Theological Seminary, Dr. W. T. Purkiser once wrote on the blackboard: "The only thing worse than preaching over people's heads is not to preach at their heads at all!"

Peter did not want to leave any doubt in the people's thinking about God's truth. He preached to enlighten their minds about what God had done through Jesus Christ.

Today many Christians have no sufficient grasp of spiritual knowledge and understanding. We must get them out of the fog. One fellow was asked, "What do you believe?"

He replied nonchalantly: "I believe the same as my church!"

"What does your church believe?" the inquirer pressed.

Quickly he answered: "The church believes just like me!"

It's no wonder one man said he "joined the church on 'confusion of faith!'"

"Then Peter stood up with the Eleven, raised his voice and addressed the crowd" (Acts 2:14). The Greek word for "raised" means he enunciated clearly! He articulated so everyone could understand! Peter's sermon could be summarized in these few words: "The signs came from the Holy Spirit; the Holy Spirit came through Jesus; Jesus could confer the Holy Spirit because He is Lord and Christ."[2]

A pattern for apostolic preaching is introduced by Peter which appears consistently throughout the Book of

---

2. LaSor, *Church Alive,* p. 47.

Acts. Apostolic preaching was always positive, explaining how far God has gone in order to bring men to himself. The progression of apostolic preaching follows four main ideas.

First, the life and Crucifixion of Jesus is presented. William Barclay writes: "The Cross was no accident. It belonged to the eternal plan of God." Peter said, "Jesus of Nazareth was a man accredited by God to you by miracles, wonders and signs, which God did among you through him, as you yourselves know. This man was handed over to you by God's set purpose and foreknowledge; and you, with the help of wicked men, put him to death by nailing him to the cross" (Acts 2:22-23). Barclay continues: "The Cross is not a kind of emergency measure flung out by God when everything else had failed. It is part of the very life of God. . . . We must never think that anything Jesus did changed the attitude of God to men. We must never set a gentle loving Jesus over against an angry, vengeful God. It was *by God* Jesus was sent."[3]

It is important to note: "The mere fact that Jesus died would save no one. It is the fact that He died according to the Scriptures, . . . according to the will of God. This was God's appointed way of saving the world. Christ's blood was shed for our sins, not just because it was His blood, but because this was the Father's will. There was no other way. And to prove that this was so, God raised Him from the dead."[4] That brings us to the second step in apostolic preaching.

Second, the resurrection of Christ, as the great proof of His Messiahship, is highlighted. Peter said, "But God raised him from the dead, freeing him from the agony of death, because it was impossible for death to keep its hold on him" (Acts 2:24).

3. William Barclay, "The Acts of the Apostles," *The Daily Study Bible* (Philadelphia: The Westminster Press, 1953), pp. 21-22.

4. LaSor, *Church Alive*, p. 50.

Ray Stedman has remarked:

> The strange and remarkable thing about Peter's sermon is that not a single voice was lifted in protest. To me one of the greatest proofs of the resurrection of Jesus is that Peter could stand up in the city were these events had taken place a little more than a month before and tell these people that Jesus had risen from the dead, with not a single person challenging Him. They knew that the authorities could not produce the body of Jesus, though they would have given a king's ransom to be able to do so . . . they stand in mute and stricken silence as the Apostle drives home with powerful strokes the sword of the Spirit, convicting them of the truth of his claim.[5]

A third point of apostolic preaching was the testimony of the Old Testament scriptures referring to Jesus as Messiah. Quotations concerning Jesus' ascension, the coming of the Holy Spirit, and of Christ as Lord of all were presented. The apostles knew and used the scriptures!

Fourth, the apostles always made an exhortation to come to repentance and to have faith. The door of salvation was open to all. There is the universal invitation, "every one of you." There is the universal condition, "repent and be baptized . . . in the name of Jesus Christ." There is the universal provision, "so that your sins may be forgiven" (Acts 2:38).

Pentecost Makes an Appeal to the Emotions—
It Stirs the Heart

God's truth goes beyond cold facts and unmoving, calculated plans. The Bible is related to real life: "The word of God is living and active. Sharper than any double-edged sword, it penetrates even to dividing soul and spirit,

---

5. Stedman, *Birth of the Body*, p. 51.

joints and marrow; it judges the thoughts and attitudes of the heart" (Heb. 4:12).

An African woman, sitting outside her hut reading the Bible, was watched by a curious neighbor. Noticing her intense expression, he asked: "Do you know what you are reading?"

She replied: "I am not reading this Book. This Book is reading me!" The Word penetrates!

As Peter used scripture to attest to the Lordship of Jesus, "they were cut to the heart and said to Peter and the other apostles, 'Brothers, what shall we do?'" (Acts 2:37). The message had made an emotional impact! They were under the power of conviction by the Holy Spirit and they were "cut" or "pricked" (KJV) in their heart. The verb *katanysso* (translated "cut" or "pricked") means "to pierce, to sting sharply, to stun, to smite." The ancient Greek writer, Homer, used this same word to describe horses pawing the ground with their hoofs.

Being confronted with the Cross, that Pentecost audience sensed their own sins and were deeply stirred. Emotion of that sort is not to be avoided, but embraced. It is the ministry of the Holy Spirit, showing us our sins in order that we may deal with them. Such a revelation should stir us!

Martin Luther studied a certain painting of the crucifixion of Christ. Then he cried out: "My God! My God! For me, for me!" And William Booth was so stirred emotionally at the sight of drunkards in the gutters of London, he couldn't eat or sleep for a week. Even so, when we begin to feel God's truth deeply, we will shake our world too. As Dr. Louis Evans once said, "We must teach while we plead, and we must plead while we teach. We must strike for the human heart as well as for the mind!"

God's great truth must be allowed to burn itself in our

hearts before it can move us to accomplish much in the power of the Spirit.

The impact of Pentecost can never allow us to settle for a dry, uninvolved, frigid religion. It's only when the fires in a man's soul or in a church are dying down, that people begin to frown on the exuberance of joy and withdraw from the impact of old-fashioned conviction! That is when formalism puts reality into a deep freeze. That is when churches try to manufacture piety. That is when people seek out substitutes for the real thing!

Lorenzo de' Medici lived during the 16th century Italian Renaissance. He was quite a showman in the city of Florence, Italy. Being rich, Lorenzo the Magnificent endowed his city with artistic splendor and spectacular pageants. He was the leading entrepreneur and art patron.

For one of his projects, Lorenzo stages a religious pageant for Pentecost Sunday. The drama was presented in one of Florence's great churches. By ingenious special effects, he reenacted the descent of fire upon the apostles. It was too realistic! Actual fire was used and the canvas stage sets were set ablaze. The whole church burned to the ground!

Playacting with religion, trying to re-create it without the power of the Holy Spirit will destroy the church.

When Peter preached on this first "Founders' Day," he spoke of God's great truths, and it resulted in the stirring of emotions until the people cried, "Brothers, what shall we do?"

Pentecost Makes an Appeal to the Will— It Demands a Decision

The crowd was moved and stirred. Pentecost called for a decision to act.

"Peter replied: 'Repent and be baptized, every one of you, in the name of Jesus Christ so that your sins may be forgiven. And you will receive the gift of the Holy Spirit. The promise is for you and your children and for all who are far off—for all whom the Lord our God will call.'

"With many other words he warned them; and he pleaded with them, 'Save yourselves from this corrupt generation.' Those who accepted his message were baptized, and about three thousand were added to their number that day" (Acts 2:38-41).

The Christian message is not merely the presentation of great truth nor just the stirring of emotions to make people feel better. Its value is gained only when one responds with his will. Pentecost demands a decision! Those hearers wanted to know what to do!

The first step was repentance. The Bible is loaded with the call to repentance. Having been moved by the power of the Holy Spirit, one's will must respond. There must be a change of mind, a change of attitude toward God, a change of attitude toward sin in one's own life. Repentance is a "godly sorrow for sin"—a deep desire to quit rebelling against God. The Bible says, "If we confess our sins, he is faithful and just and will forgive us our sins and purify us from all unrighteousness" (1 John 1:9). Repentance is more than emotion, although it may include deep emotion. Repentance is a new direction for life. It is not a matter of feeling, but a matter of willing. As Jowett once said, "It is to lay hold of the aimless, drifting thought, and steer it toward God. It is a change of mind."

The second step is, in Peter's words: ". . . be baptized, every one of you, in the name of Jesus Christ so that your sins may be forgiven" (Acts 2:38). Repentance is not the end. According to the Bible, the new believer is to express his newfound faith in Christ by public baptism in Jesus' name. It is God's prescribed method of expressing faith in Christ. Because one has been forgiven of sins committed, he must be willing to obey God and be baptized. Only one who has repented is eligible for baptism. A sinner is not saved through baptism. Forgiveness of sins is the prerequisite for baptism.

In the very same way, baptized Christians are candidates for the gift of the Holy Spirit: "Repent and be baptized, every one of you . . . And you will receive the gift of the Holy Spirit" (Acts 2:38). There is no magic in the water, but obedience to the command of God is primary! Jesus says to each of us: "'If you love me, you will do what I command'" (John 14:15). If one doesn't love Jesus and doesn't wish to obey His commands, he should not be baptized! Baptism is one's public affirmation of trust in Christ and willingness to obey.

Luke added, "Those who accepted his message were baptized, and about three thousand were added to their number that day" (Acts 2:41).

The first time the Law was proclaimed—the day Moses came down from Mount Sinai—3,000 men were killed. But on the first occasion grace was preached—the day the Holy Spirit came down at Pentecost—3,000 were saved, baptized, and added to the Body of Christ! What a magnificent gospel!

These 3,000 were added to the 120 Spirit-filled disciples—but more importantly, they were added to Christ! Now they shared the life of Christ as does a branch share the life of the vine! To them were added the virtues of His death and the victories of His resurrection. And Christ gained 3,000 people as instruments of His love and work. The Body cannot be separated from the Head. The Church and Christ are inseparable! If a man wants Christ, he must have the Church. If he wants the Church, he must have

Christ. We are added to the Body in order to serve. More than being added to the "roll," we are added to some "role" within the Body of Christ. It is a "role" of empowered service!

The Early Church was founded upon the power of the Holy Spirit who came to cleanse, to fill, to occupy, to be President of men's hearts. The Church was founded to tell men of the availability of the Holy Spirit, who enables believers to live clean lives, holy lives, empowered lives. The Church must give itself to great boldness instead of great buildings, seeking great courage instead of great comfort, the dominance of the Spirit instead of the dominance of status, great power instead of great prestige!

John T. Seamands wrote: "I remember watching a TV program 'Candid Camera' a few years ago. A woman coasted downhill in a car and rolled into a filling station. 'Fill it up with regular,' she said to the smiling attendant, 'and check the oil, please.'

"Imagine the look of astonishment on the man's face when he lifted up the hood and found there was no engine! The Church in many places reminds me of a car that has lost its engine. It has lost its source of power."[6]

With New Testament in his hand, an Indian Hindu asked a missionary: "Sir, I read in the New Testament's Book of Acts that the disciples of Jesus received a mighty baptism with the Holy Spirit. My question to you is this: Sir, have you received this baptism?"

Like so many well-meaning Christians, the missionary was ignorant of the baptism of the Holy Spirit. He was honest, however, and began seeking in prayer and study. In answer to his quest, God filled him with the Holy Spirit and he became an effective witness for Jesus Christ. But,

---

6. John T. Seamands, *On Tiptoe with Love* (Kansas City: Beacon Hill Press of Kansas City, 1971), p. 56.

this question must be answered: "Sir, have *you* received this baptism?"[7]

The baptism of the Spirit was not just for the day of the founders. Peter declared: "The promise is for you and your children and for all who are far off" (Acts 2:39). When we make our personal surrender, any room can be our Upper Room, and any day our Day of Pentecost!

7. William M. Greathouse, *The Fullness of the Spirit* (Kansas City: Nazarene Publishing House, 1958), pp. 51-52.

CHAPTER 6

Climate for Change

Acts 2:42-47

Gene Autry, well-known cowboy of other days, and now owner of the California Angels baseball team, said of the rival Los Angeles Dodgers' president: "There's nothing in the world I wouldn't do for O'Malley. There's nothing he wouldn't do for me. That's the way it is. We go through life doing nothing for each other."

That's the climate of the world's philosophy: "I won't do to you what I don't want you to do to me!" At best, it is a religious standoff! Men go through life doing nothing for each other!

The empowered Church, from the Day of Pentecost, could never settle for the "live and let live" approach to life. There was an aura about the Early Church which induced men to undergo fantastic change! Old patterns and defiling habits were broken. New values paced the new life in Christ! Guilt was gone! The sinful past no longer chained men's lives to the lowlands! The Spirit of God produced spiritual revolutions in those who allowed Jesus to be their Lord and Master! In such a climate of acceptance, people shed the carnal nature of the soul and put on the "new man" nature of Christ. The atmosphere of the early Christians was transformed from gloom to gladness and glory! The sweet Spirit of God drew more followers than the prophets of doom.

It is profitable to look at the Church before well-meaning men made Christianity so complicated. It was the Church launched at Pentecost which provided a climate for change!

The Church Had a Climate of Expectancy

Luke wrote: "They devoted themselves to the apostles' teaching and to the fellowship, to the breaking of bread and to prayer. Everyone was filled with awe, and many wonders and miracles were done by the apostles" (Acts 2:42-43).

The Christians devoted themselves to the apostles' teaching. The content of apostolic teaching was, at first, from the firsthand reports shared by actual witnesses of Jesus' life and ministry. It was delivered with authority, because it was the Lord's teaching orally communicated through the apostles. With the passing of time, the apostles' teaching took written form, culminating in our New Testament. This body of doctrine, known as the *didache*, was the basic content needed for spiritual growth in the power of the Spirit.

When a man came to the church in those days, his motive was simply: "What more can I learn about Christ and Christianity?" The firsthand preaching of the apostles was his chief source of information.

Some of the older versions of Acts say the believers "persevered" in the apostles' teaching. It reminds us of Jesus' earlier words: "'If you hold to my teaching, you are

74

really my disciples'" (John 8:31). One can recognize Christ's follower by his appetite for truth. He has an awakened mind. There is so much to learn, to relearn, to think through. Conversion awakens the mind for the acceptance of spiritual truth!

Too many modern Christians don't know what they believe! Often what they believe is little more than popular notions tinged with Christian emotion! The believer must give himself to the study of God's Word if he is to be equipped for this day!

The first-century Christians devoted themselves to the fellowship of believers. There was no element of an every-man-doing-what-was-right-in-his-own-eyes concept in the Early Church. Spiritual anarchy can never produce Christian unity! If we think, "It's every man for himself," then the devil gets the whole bunch! These early Christians were drawn together in fellowship because their hearts were awakened. They were noted for their mutual love and respect. It was a fellowship known as *koinonia*.

Koinonia fellowship is based on one's fellowship with the Holy Spirit. That's where real dynamic fellowship begins. Without the Spirit's control, we are stuck together—not melted together in love. Spiritual communion and fellowship is more than the herd instinct of our humanity. It is supernatural—given by the Spirit.

A lot of church "fellowship" is no more spiritual communion than the local Kiwanis or Rotary club meeting. Too often we remain at the friendly, fraternizing level—and you can do that without Christ or the Church. In his book *The Taste of New Wine,* Keith Miller said:

> Our churches are filled with people who outwardly look contented and at peace but inwardly are crying out for someone to love them—just as they are—confused, frustrated, often frightened, guilty, and often unable to communicate even within their own families.

But the *other* people in the church *look* so happy and contented that one seldom has the courage to admit his own deep needs before such a self-sufficient group as the average church meeting appears to be.[1]

That describes the church without *koinonia* fellowship!

Another author states it well:

> The *koinonia* of the Holy Spirit is that fellowship of believers which the Holy Spirit gives. It is precisely that experience of a deeper communion, of a supernatural intercommunication, that perhaps every believer occasionally has felt in the presence of other believers. Its basis is the oneness that Christians share in Christ. A shared faith, a shared salvation and a shared divine nature are the roots of *koinonia*. The basic idea of the word *koinonia* is, in fact, that of something held in common.[2]

We are bonded together as believers into "one body and one Spirit—just as you were called to one hope when you were called—one Lord, one faith, one baptism; one God and Father of all, who is over all and through all in all" (Eph. 4:4-6).

The Church becomes the center where lonely people find friends, where sinners find understanding and forgiveness, and where Christians get help from those who have common belief. Dr. E. Stanley Jones says this kind of fellowship exerts a pressure on you in the right direction. You soon discover you can't let your friends down. Because they expect so much of you, you tend to live up to their expectations. It's a conspiracy of love to make everyone come up to his best!

---

1. Keith Miller, *The Taste of New Wine* (Waco, Tex.: Word Books), p. 22.

2. Howard A. Snyder, *The Problem of Wine Skins* (Downers Grove, Ill.: Inter-Varsity Press, 1975), p. 93.

Marian Parrish told this beautiful story: "I was struggling to know how to relate to a young woman who had recently lost her baby, as well as the opportunity to ever give birth again. I dialed my friend's number, and as I waited for her to answer the telephone, I cast about for something interesting to talk about. We were taking a trip—I could tell her about that! I had recently met a well-known preacher—that might interest her.

"Then my friend answered, and I heard myself saying, 'I just wanted to tell you how much I care about you.'

"From the warm conversation that followed, I knew I had made the right choice. Perhaps the most interesting thing we can ever reveal about ourselves to another person is that we care."[3]

In the climate of expectancy, the early Christians devoted themselves to breaking of bread. It appears the reference here is to the Lord's Supper instituted on the eve of Jesus' crucifixion. Jesus had instructed them that night as He broke the bread and handed it to them: "'This is my body given for you; do this in remembrance of me'" (Luke 22:19). Each participation is in anticipation of Jesus' final return and Lordship. The believers are drawn like a family to the dinner table as they break bread together.

Also, with expectancy, the Christians devoted themselves to prayer. Prayer became a vital link in their continuing fellowship with God and with each other. We are strongest as we unite in prayer. Too much prayer is just an emergency measure instead of a way of life.

The airplane pilot grabbed his microphone and said: "Pilot to tower—pilot to tower! I am 300 miles from land—

---

3. Marian Parrish in an article in *Guideposts* magazine (November, 1972), p. 6.

600 feet high and running out of gas. Please instruct. Over."

A voice came back: "Tower to pilot—tower to pilot. Repeat after me: 'Our Father which art in heaven . . .'"

The Early Church had more than just an emergency connection. They were strengthened by prayer. People who pray for each other can survive the things which threaten to divide them. There's a powerful unity among Christians who band together in prayer.

The Church gathered to do the basics of Christian survival: hearing God's Word spoken, sharing the fellowship, breaking the bread of Communion, and praying in the power of the Spirit. Such a climate of expectancy added another dimension.

The Church Had a Climate of Exchange

The Acts account continues: "All the believers were together and had everything in common. Selling their possessions and goods, they gave to anyone as he had need" (Acts 2:44-45).

All believers were together. Wherever one saw a disciple, he would see more—like birds of a feather flocking together! To sustain that vital sense of unity, there must be time for all believers to be together. The church is always in danger of segmenting into groups and subgroups at the expense of the whole Body of Christ.

All believers had everything in common. There was such a willingness to help each other it was said: they had all things in common—according to the law of friendship. Some have tried to twist this incident into a New Testament communism. Nothing could be farther from the truth. A close study reveals basic differences:

1. The impulse is love, not force.

2. This sharing sprang from faith in God, not a denial of God.

3. This action was voluntary, not an obligation.

4. The people who participated were the Church, not enemies of the Church.

For centuries before Pentecost, Jews were required to come to Jerusalem for the three solemn feasts each year. There was always a sort of community of goods. During those special festivals, pilgrims were given housing or beds free of charge. Often the household utensils—ovens, caldrons, tables, spits, etc., were made available. Adequate water was supplied at public expense. A sort of community of goods was no strange thing in Jerusalem at such times.

To some commentators it appears that with the remarkable events of this particular Pentecost, the outpouring of the Holy Spirit and conversions taking place, these people lingered in Jerusalem longer than originally planned, and the activity described in verses 44-45 was initiated during the days immediately following Pentecost. It may have continued for an unknown length of time. They formed a kind of temporary community to provide for everyone's needs. Some sold their possessions to help defray the added costs of this unusual "camp meeting" which launched the Church of Jesus Christ.

All believers gave sacrificially. There was no force, no holding back—just spontaneous giving to help temporary human needs. This was above their regular tithes paid faithfully at the Temple.

One deacon said to his pastor: "Money is not important. If the people are committed to Christ and to one another, they can do anything they are supposed to do as a church!"

One of my parishioners, Bob Grant, gave a good definition of sacrifice: "Sacrifice is giving up something in exchange for something better!" There's nothing we can give God that is anywhere near what we have received from God's hand. To have God's presence, His smile of approval is more valuable than anything one could possibly "sacrifice" for God.

All believers shared with those who had need. It's a hard lesson to learn, that what people ask for is not always what they need (see Acts 3).

One fellow said, "A panhandler came up to me and said he hadn't had a bite in two weeks."

His friend replied: "Poor fellow! What did you do?"

"I bit him, of course!"

Where Christians have need, God has friends who can readily respond. The Church expands in the climate of exchange—an atmosphere of sharing.

The Church Had a Climate of Encouragement

Author Luke notes: "Every day they continued to meet together in the temple courts. They broke bread in their homes and ate together with glad and sincere hearts, praising God and enjoying the favor of all the people" (Acts 2:46-47).

The disciples continued to meet together publicly at the place of worship. The King James Version translates it: "They, continuing daily with one accord in the temple . . ." (v. 46). It's one thing to get a bunch of Christians in one place—but it's something else to get them in one place "with one accord"—in the same mind. It's a harmony of soul and spirit—one note!

The author has played in symphony orchestras located in cities where he has been a pastor. Before a symphony concert, each player rehearses rather freely, going up and down scales and running over difficult passages in the musical score. The result is a cacophony of sound—

audio chaos! Along comes the concertmaster, the leader of the first violin section. He gets his pitch from the oboe. All confusion stops. Each member of the orchestra listens carefully and then tunes his own instrument to the concertmaster's note.

Silence! In walks the maestro, the conductor. Under his direction the collection of 70 or 80 instruments combine to produce beautiful melody and harmony—a blending of all the voices of the various instruments. All follow the direction of the master! In so doing, each musician plays in accord with all the others. The sound is magic—inspiring, uplifting!

Worship is a time to celebrate, to atune ourselves to Christ, to join our hearts and voices in public praise of Him who alone is worthy to be praised! Allow Him to be Master—bringing out the best in us!

Jesus' friends must be friends to each other. A church without fellowship is like a world without people. The Church today may have great cathedrals in which to worship—but, if there is no fellowship, the cathedral is a tomb! Keith Huttenlocker has said:

> A popular synidcated columnist often reminds his readers that each of us wears a button on his chest which says: I want to feel important. The Church ought to be a place where indeed *everyone* feels important. . . . We do not need to make anyone *feel* important. Everyone *is* important. If we would awaken to that fact we would overlook none. We would belittle none. If anyone is a member of the church he is one ransomed by Christ's death.[4]

A traveler in a European village discovered a beautiful custom. At night she saw the people going to church, each carrying a little bronze lamp. These lamps were placed in

---

4. Keith Huttenlocker, *Love Makes the Word Go Round* (Anderson, Ind.: Warner Press, 1974), pp. 26-27.

sockets by the family pew. The soft light of the lamps was the only lighting for the service. If a member was absent, there was a dark place.

When we are absent from the fellowship and celebration, we leave darkness in our place. As we join together, there is the glow of inspiration unequalled in any other way.

When one participates in corporate worship, he avails himself of the healing powers of Christian fellowship. The term *disciple* is used in the New Testament approximately 230 times before Pentecost and only 28 times after. By contrast, the term *brother* is used approximately 30 times before, and more than 230 times after Pentecost. Real discipleship leads to brotherhood!

In the climate of encouragement, the Christians broke bread together in their homes with "glad and sincere hearts, praising God and enjoying the favor of all the people" (Acts 2:46-47). No snobbery, no superiority, no destructive complexes, no intolerance, no temperamental excesses—just breaking bread with each other as symbolic of a joyful fellowship. Even the commonplace became special! Plain ordinary bread-breaking became a festival of gladness!

This note of encouragement came from sincere hearts. The word Luke used to describe "sincere" originally meant, "free from stones or rocks." Those warmhearted Christians held no hardness of heart, no impediments to love—just evenness and purity!

A sign on a radiator in a hotel room said: "Please turn the radiators all the way on or all the way off. If they are turned only partially on, they will leak and be noisy." There are too many Christians who are squeaky and noisy. All their joy and gladness leaks away! Why? They are turned on just halfway—they have just enough religion to be unhappy!

But not these fellows from Pentecost! They were really turned on by the power of the Holy Spirit! As they broke bread together, they praised God because things were happening between them, in them, and through them!

In an empowered Church things still happen. A man who had been a drunkard and ruined his life and his family, became a Christian one wonderful day, and God helped him to conquer his terrible drinking habit. He became a good husband, father, and citizen. Some fellows at work teased him once, saying, "Hey, you don't believe in the Bible and all those miracles, do you? You don't believe Jesus turned water into wine and all those stories, do you?"

The new Christian answered: "I'm no scholar, and I can't debate whether or not Jesus turned water into wine, but in my house I've seen Him change alcohol into furniture and clothing and good food!"

Our God is still able to change people! Through His Church that has a climate of expectancy, a climate of exchange, a climate of encouragement, He will perform miracles of love and grace!

E. Stanley Jones wrote this classic paragraph:

Hitherto men thought that goodness was the exceptional achievement of the exceptional man; but here the ordinary garden variety of humanity found a contagious, powerful type of goodness that transformed the face of humanity. And they found it, not as the whipping up of the will in a strained effort at goodness, but as a relaxed spontaneity from within. Goodness became their native air, the natural output. They were naturalized in contagious goodness. This opened up such an astonishing possibility to morally beaten humanity that multitudes flocked into this new Fellowship where anything that was right was possible. A strange, sober joy went across that sad and decaying world—joy that goodness was here for the asking, that moral victory was possible now, that guilt could be lifted from the stricken conscience, that inner conflict could be resolved and inner unity found, that the total person could be heightened and a "plus" added to one, and that a Fellowship of like-souled persons gave one a sense of belonging. It was Good News. And it worked![5]

5. Jones, *Way to Power and Poise*, p. 28.

CHAPTER 7

Keep Right: God at Work

Acts 3 :1-11

In Acts 1 the Holy Spirit is promised. In Acts 2 the Holy Spirit is outpoured. In Acts 3 the Holy Spirit is at work! Luke begins to close his second chapter with: "Everyone was filled with awe, and many wonders and miracles were done by the apostles" (Acts 2:43). Acts 3 opens with Luke selecting one of these miracles to explain in more detail. It happens to be a miracle which sets in motion a chain of events.

Twelve centuries later, Thomas Aquinas was visiting Pope Innocent IV in Rome. The Pope showed him the vast treasuries in the church's vaults. Pointing to the hoard of wealth, Pope Innocent IV remarked: "No longer can the church say, 'Silver and gold have I none.'"

Thomas Aquinas replied, "It's true, Holy Father, nor can she say to the lame man, 'Rise up and walk.'"

A church can be poor but powerful, and, unfortunately, a church can also be a rich corpse! Church history is the tragic account of the rise and fall between the dynamic of the Holy Spirit and the decay caused by the secular spirit. However, H. G. Wells, a noted agnostic historian, wrote:

> We must remember that through all those ages, leaving profound consequences, but leaving no conspicuous records upon the historian's page, countless men and women were touched by that Spirit of Jesus which still lived and lives still at the core of Christianity, that they led lives that were on the whole gracious and helpful, and that they did unselfish and devoted deeds. through those ages such lives cleared the air, and made a better world possible.[1]

On America's highways are temporary signs which say: "Keep right: men at work." One doesn't stop or quit altogether. With caution the stream of traffic moves right ahead while workmen build or make needed repairs.

During this era of the Holy Spirit, initiated at the Day of Pentecost, there's a sign on the road of our pilgrimage: "Keep right: God at work." He continues to build and repair and salvage and rebuild His Church. We must not quit or abandon hope, but keep right on in the stream of the Spirit. Thank the Lord, God is at work—even today!

God Is at Work in the Commonplaces of Life

Luke records in his third chapter of Acts: "One day Peter and John were going up to the temple at the time of prayer—at three in the afternoon" (Acts 3:1). Here is a subtle lesson that in the ordinary situations of life, God produces the extraordinary.

God is with us in ordinary days. The Day of Pentecost had passed. The tongues of fire were but memories. The mighty rushing wind sound was now hushed. The ecstasy

---

1. H. G. Wells, *The Outline of History,* Vol. 2 (Garden City, N.Y.: Garden City Books, 1956), p. 525.

of that event had subsided. The unique revival had flared with its flaming fire, but now life goes on in its normal course—and that is when God intended to start the building processes of His Church. The idea of perpetual "revival" is a contradiction of the terms and purposes for which God designed us. He wants to do the miraculous, not on high mountain experiences, but in the dust of our workaday world.

God is with us in our usual places. Peter and John were walking through the streets and courtyards and marketplaces of Jerusalem. Going to the Temple as usual, they passed through the commonplaces of life where God wants to bring virtue and victory.

The late Dr. Hugh C. Benner, the man who laid hands on the author at his ordination ceremony, said: "So far as the record goes, not one soul was converted in the Upper Room. . . . We must get out of the 'Upper Rooms' out to where the needy are waiting, and give them our witness to the redeeming love and grace and power of Jesus Christ."[2]

> *I sought to hear the voice of God*
> *And climbed the topmost steeple:*
> *But God declared: "Go down again—*
> *I dwell among the people."*
> —JOHN HENRY NEWMAN

God is with us in our routine disciplines of the faith. Peter and John were going as usual to the Temple to worship and pray and give their tithes. At the ninth hour, approximately three o'clock in the afternoon, was the routine time for prayer by the Jews. For the Christians that hour had special significance: at three o'clock in the afternoon, Jesus died on the Cross—exactly the same time when the sacrificial lamb was slaughtered each day.

2. Hugh C. Benner, *The Church in Mission* (Kansas City: Beacon Hill Press of Kansas City, 1976), p. 7.

The disciplines of regular worship and daily prayer and consistent tithing may seem mundane at times, but these are the channels for many of God's miracles. God is with us in these important exercises and disciplines of our faith. Impotent Christians are undisciplined in these areas, and it reflects all through their anemic experience and witness.

Each day God makes appointments for every Christian. Do you recognize and keep them? Or, are you waiting until some great moment comes your way? Only as we keep our regular disciplines are we equipped for the great moments.

God Is at Work Through Spirit-filled Men

Continuing Luke's narration: "Peter and John were going up to the temple. . . . Now a man crippled from birth was being carried to the temple gate called Beautiful, where he was put every day to beg from those going into the temple courts" (Acts 3:1-2). The gate called Beautiful is believed to be the Nicanor gate between the Court of the Gentiles and the Court of the Women. Josephus indicated it was made of Corinthian brass and plated with gold and silver, standing about 75 feet high and 60 feet wide!

"When he [the lame beggar] saw Peter and John about to enter, he asked them for money. Peter looked straight at him, as did John" (Acts 3:3-4).

God works through men and women who are sensitive to people in need. The beggar "asked them for money." The Greek imperfect tense means, "he kept asking them!" Peter and John couldn't ignore him. Since they had come under the Holy Spirit's control, they saw others as human beings, not as "bits of junk!" The King James Version says Peter "fastened his eyes on him." He couldn't help but give full attention to the poor crippled beggar.

Christians can never get over suffering humanity. Norman Vincent Peale admired his preacher father. He studied long hours, worked hard, and he loved people. Dr. Peale has often related an incident about his father; "One time I found him sitting on a curbstone in Columbus, sobbing. 'Dad, what in the world is wrong with you?' I asked.

"'I've been out visiting the people and their sorrows and troubles break my heart.' I sat down on the curb beside him, put my arm around him. Always later I hoped that God would give me that much love for people."

God can use men who are sensitive to the troubled and lost of our world. Miracles can happen through compassionate people.

William Booth, founder of the Salvation Army, at one meeting saw hundreds packed into the capacity of the auditorium. One of his aides, Lt. Col. William Haines, rejoiced to him: "General, it's wonderful! Did you see them? Around 100 came forward to repent in just 10 minutes!"

Booth was sombre: "But I saw hundreds going out, having rejected Christ!" Booth was always haunted by the person lost in his sins!

God works through men who are not afraid to be identified with Jesus. "Peter looked straight at him, as did John. Then Peter said, 'Look at us!' So the man gave them his attention, expecting to get something from them" (Acts 3:4-5). There is something moving in Peter's audacity to be able to say: "Look on us!" (v. 4, KJV). In other words, "Do you need help? Do you need an answer? Do you want to see what God can do for a fellow? Then look at us!"

One must ask himself: "Am I ready to live like that? Am I willing to be unashamedly identified as a product of God's grace? If not, why not?" Paul wrote to the Corinthian people: "Therefore I urge you to imitate me" (1 Cor. 4:16). To young Timothy, Paul said, "Don't let anyone look down on you because you are young, but set an example for the believers in speech, in life, in love, in faith, and in purity" (1 Tim. 4:12).

Peter has come through the school of faith and he can say with confidence: "Look on us!" Kenneth Chafin expressed it well: "There are so few people in this world who really care for people that the church will meet with far greater response than it thinks—as long as it does not intend to manipulate or use people. When the church is willing to be an instrument of love, love-starved people will respond."

God works through men who have freely received and willingly give. "Then Peter said, 'I have no silver or gold, but what I have I give you'" (Acts 3:6). That simple word *I have* means in the Greek text, "That which I hold or possess!" The Church can only give what it has received from the Lord. As W. E. McCumber editorialized: "In the same way, if the church lacks life, peace, and freedom, then the church cannot give life, peace, and freedom to a world dead in its sins, troubled by its guilt, and shackled by its ignorance of the truth. Nothing is sadder than a broken world when it is confronted by a bankrupt church."[3] We have received freely from the Lord and let's be quick to give it away!

A group of natives in East Africa walked many miles past a government hospital to come to the mission hospital for treatment. Someone at the government institution asked why they had walked the extra distance to go to the mission. They replied, "The medicines may be the same, but the hands are different!"

---

3. W. E. McCumber, "I Have . . . I Give," *Herald of Holiness* (November 1, 1977), p. 16.

Henry Wadsworth Longfellow wrote: "Give what you have. To someone, it may be better than you dare to think."

Dr. McCumber added in his *Herald of Holiness* editorial: "A great thing about this giving is the fact that the giver is not diminished. God gives to people His Spirit, but He remains the all-powerful God. The apostles gave strength to the beggar, but are not themselves weakened in doing so. If you give money you are poor by the amount you give. But if you channel the resources of the name of Jesus into the lives of others, both they and you are enriched! But before we can give, we must ourselves receive."[4]

A little girl cut some flowers and took them to a sick neighbor. She came back jumping with joy over the delight of sharing. When she started to wash her hands after handling the cut flowers, her mother said: "Smell your hands first!" The fragrant odor of the flowers lingered on her hands. "Always remember," the mother said, "the fragrance of what you give away always stays with you!"

God works through men who admit personal bankruptcy but who are amazingly adequate in the Spirit of God. Peter announced: "Silver and gold have I none; but such as I have give I thee" (v. 6, KJV). There may be an absence of money, but there was the presence of power! "Such as I have give I thee!" That is a Christian's philosophy of life!

During a worship service an old man put a small slip of paper into the offering plate. The paper had the message: "I will pray one hour a day!"

It turned out that the old man's wife had died after a long and expensive illness. He had been forced to sell his home to pay medical bills. Now he was living with his

---

4. *Ibid.*

married daughter. He explained: "I'm too old to work and I haven't any money. But I can pray. So each week I bring my pledge to God and to His people."

When we give what we have, no gift is too small or insignificant. God will use it in a special way!

An American tourist watched a missionary nurse applying medicine to the open wound of a leper. The sight was a shocking one—revolting to the eye and stomach! He said to her: "I wouldn't do that for a million dollars!"

The Christian nurse smiled: "Neither would I!"

"Silver and gold have I none; but such as I have give I thee!"

God Is at Work to Help Human Need

Concealed in the Greek text are several words from Luke's medical vocabulary. Being a physician, Luke uses medical terms to describe the beggar's feet, anklebones, and his leaping action. These particular words were not used elsewhere in the New Testament, but are the technical terms of a man schooled in human need. Here was a man crippled from a congenital disease.

Peter commanded: "In the name of Jesus Christ of Nazareth, walk" (Acts 3:6).

God gives what is needed, not what is asked! It's true Jesus once said, "Everyone who asks receives" (Matt. 7:8). But when God takes over by His grace, we often get more than we ask! That beggar asked for a handout, but he got health instead!

In the power of the Spirit, Peter said, "Walk!" He used the present tense, meaning, "Start walking and keep on walking!" This was not to be a single moment only; not just a step and all is over. God gave a healing touch which could *keep* him walking.

92

The beggar had a predictable response: he just sat there. After all, he knew he couldn't walk. He probably considered himself an authority on ankles—he had watched people walk for years. A fellow can know much about ankles, however, and still not know how to walk! Asking for money, he was expecting too little!

His hope of improvement reminds me of an incident in an old church building. There weren't enough classrooms to go around, so one of the children's classes was crowded into the furnace room. When a little girl heard a new church was being built, she asked: "Will we have a bigger furnace room in the new church?"

Peter was saying to the beggar: "I don't have anything to give you that will maintain you while you are a cripple—but I have something to cure your condition! I can't give you money, but I'll make you able to earn your own living!"

The Church was not born to dole out to people who are capable of doing something better! It was born to put people on their feet and enable them to do without begging. As William LaSor commented: "We do not have money to keep you in your present condition, but we do have something to get you out of this condition." Our message is one of releasing God's redemptive work here on this earth!

God gives miracles of grace through Jesus' name. Peter said, "In the name of Jesus Christ of Nazareth, walk!" There's power in the name of Jesus! Peter was depending upon the authority and resources of Jesus to work a miracle.

At Texas Instruments Incorporated in Dallas, miraculous discoveries and techniques in electronics are taking place. Scores of electronic components are squeezed through a flake of alum crystal so small it can slip through the eye of a needle. There's a sign on the wall: "We do not believe in miracles; we rely on them!"

Nowhere should that be more true than where God's people work and pray in the name of Jesus—we must rely on miracles of grace! Jesus made this amazing promise: "Anyone who has faith in me will do what I have been doing. He will do even greater things than these, because I am going to the Father. And I will do whatever you ask in my name, so that the Son may bring glory to the Father. You may ask me for anything in my name, and I will do it" (John 14:12-14).

God gives a helping hand through His people. "Taking him by the right hand, he [Peter] helped him up, and instantly the man's feet and ankles became strong. He jumped to his feet and began to walk" (Acts 3:7-8). What a calling! To lift the downcast! To be in partnership with God in lifting and raising up people! Take them by the hand with that personal, direct contact!

The church which stands afar off from human need, in huddles of humility, merely mocks the heartache of the helpless! We must get right down alongside the wounded, weary world and hold out the right hand of healing and help. That is how Christ chooses to make living contact— through His people. We are to lift a broken world to its feet!

William P. Barker wrote:

> A pastor of a congregation in the slums once told a group of solicitous suburban churchmen, "We don't want your food baskets at Christmas, or your old clothes and your cast-off toys. We don't want your offers to send paint to fix up our church basement. We want *you*. We need *you*. We would like to know that you care. That's what you can give us!" . . .
>
> He intends us to touch the shrivelled, dying community around us with the vitality given only by the Living Jesus Christ.[5]

---

5. Barker, *They Stood Boldly,* p. 35.

God gives reason to rejoice! "He jumped to his feet and began to walk. Then he went with them into the temple courts, walking and jumping, and praising God. When all the people saw him walking and praising God, they recognized him as the same man who used to sit begging at the temple gate called Beautiful, and they were filled with wonder and amazement at what had happened to him" (Acts 3:8-10).

The beggar had been touched not only in body, but in soul. He was "walking, leaping, and praising God!" He experienced something better than silver and gold! And the first place he went was right into the Temple—jumping up and down, overjoyed and grateful to God! As McCumber says, "No longer at the gate begging, he is now *through* the gate, worshipping!"

His jubilant praise brought new life and excitement into the Temple service that day! Everyone was blessed by the wonderful miracle of grace. Joy swept through the Temple as that new man in Christ shouted praises to God! I believe God's touch brings joy.

Recently I was with a group of people discussing various modes of expression in worship. In the group was a lady who acted like a talent scout for a cemetery! Her negative conversation scathed people who shout or express praise to God with any enthusiasm in public worship. She thought it deplorable that anyone have a religion which made them expressive and happy.

Unable to resist, I told about the man who kept interrupting the gloomy atmosphere of a dead church by saying, "Amen! Well, praise the Lord!"

Finally an usher came to him: "You must keep quiet."

The old man said, "I'm sorry, but I just can't hold it in. I've got a wonderful religion!"

The usher intoned: "Well, you didn't get it here!"

The happy beggar in Luke's story unknowingly fulfilled an Old Testament prophecy describing the age of the Messiah: "Then shall the lame man leap as an hart" (Isa. 35:6, KJV). Yes, he had reason to sing and shout and praise God.

The mighty works of God are often very personal, but nonetheless significant and real.

During the invitation at the close of a morning service, a little boy, seven years of age, came to the altar to give his heart to Jesus. Next to him knelt his concerned parents. With his arm around his son, the father prayed, "Thank You, Lord, for saving my boy!"

Others may have gone out the back door thinking, "Oh, just a little boy went forward. That's not much of a response to an invitation!" But it's what happens to you or a little boy at the altar that makes it a mighty work of God!

George Buttrick expressed it like this:

> There once was a time when God saw the world lying like a cripple on the doorstep of heaven. God had something that He could not keep. That was His own life and love. The beggar asked only for alms and a cooling drink, but God gave him a Baby to love, a Man to follow, and a Life to adore, a Spirit to dwell in his own wretched, crippled body and make him walk, and leap, and praise again.[6]

And there is a healing touch for one's life today! Whatever has crippled one's spirit, broken one's life, or bound one with regret and bitterness, can be released this moment in the power of Jesus' name. The challenge to all is: Rise up and walk! And keep on walking in the power of the Holy Spirit!

---

6. Buttrick, *Interpreter's Bible,* 9:35.

CHAPTER 8

Trusting, Not Trying

Acts 3:11-26

The lame beggar had not improved because he tried harder; his miraculous healing came as a result of trusting. The atmosphere was electric with praise and joy. The former lame beggar hung onto Peter and John as he shouted with delight for God's touch of health and wholeness. People came running from every direction to get in on the excitement. Robert Louis Stevenson has written: "I care not for your prayers; let me see your praise!" And that's what drew the crowd!

Peter, being a preacher at heart, couldn't face such a large audience without giving a sermon. Amid the exuberance of newfound joy, the clamoring of the curious, Peter spoke of the new life offered through Jesus Christ. This new life in Christ is not our natural life at its highest point of attainment, the result of trying real hard. It is the divine life brought down to the lowest point where it touches the hearts of fallen men. It is the simple childlike trust in God's integrity and love. God's life is poured into men, not as a result of turning over a new leaf, but as an invasion of love from above.

Peter makes four important points concerning the new life in Christ.

God Is the Source of New Life

Peter began his masterful message: "Men of Israel, why does this surprise you? Why do you stare at us as if by our own power or godliness we had made this man walk? The God of Abraham, Isaac and Jacob, the God of our fathers, has glorified his servant Jesus" (Acts 3:12-13).

Apparently Peter recognized he was speaking to Jews. The many visitors that had flooded Jerusalem for the holidays had gone back to their various provinces and countries. The apostle, standing before the wondering crowd, looked around and said, "Men of Israel, why does this surprise you? Why do you stare at us?" In other words, "Of all people, you should know better! You ought to know that God is like this! For centuries God has been at work on your behalf! Why are you surprised?"

Peter continued: "Why do you stare at us as if by our own power or godliness we had made this man walk?" One wonders if we might have been tempted to say: "We sure worked a long time to see this finally happen!" Or, "We belong to a great church!" But Peter and John assume no personal greatness. Their only authority is the authority of Jesus Christ. Before Pentecost and their infilling with the Holy Spirit, one might have expected Peter to jump into the spotlight and give the typical politician's victory wave to the crowds. But not now! Peter knows full well his own power or godliness had nothing to do with the miraculous healing of the lame beggar. Peter's reluctance to gain praise for himself is another proof of God's transforming power!

The source of this new life is God the Father! We can do many religious things without God's help. We can fill Sunday school buses; make the classes interesting and cheerfully decorated; give good instruction, lifting the manners and ideals of the people; and raise their moral goals. All of this can be done without God. Churches can have attractive and spacious buildings, a good organ and choir, many fellowship groups, an eloquent pulpiteer, and have special programs and spectacular musicals—all without God! But, if we crave to see men and women born again into the kingdom of God, moved to repentance, desperate enough to bow before God, to have a real life-changing faith, then we *must* have God! He must be the motivation for all we do—whether in the church program or our personal ministry. He is the only source of power to bring broken hearts and lives into Christ's new life.

Paul may plant and Apollos may water, but one must never forget that God alone gives the increase! When we have done our very best, it is still inadequate apart from God's power! He is our ever-present source of power!

Our love for God falters! We speak on His behalf with only stammering lips. We don't have power or godliness in ourselves that could save anybody or anything. If we thought we had power, we might trust in it. If we had our own righteousness, we might trust in that! As it is, we can only seek God's mercy and power. He alone is able to give new life to those seeking help.

When Robert Morrison, the first missionary to China, was leaving his ship in a Cninese port, the captain sneered at him: "So you think you are going to make an impression on China?"

Morrison replied quietly: "No, sir—but I believe God will!"

Jesus taught: "Let your light shine before men, that they may see your good deeds and praise your Father in heaven" (Matt. 5:16). John the Baptist pointed to Jesus one day and remarked: "He must become greater; I must become less important" (John 3:30). Later Paul echoed the same truth: "For we do not preach ourselves, but Jesus Christ as Lord" (2 Cor. 4:5). And Peter reminds the Temple crowd: "By faith in the name of Jesus, this man whom you see and know was made strong. It is Jesus' name and the faith that comes through him that has given this complete healing to him" (Acts 3:16).

The Risen Lord is the source of power. Peter and John were but channels of God's power. There are no limitations to what the Risen Lord can do through His people. That's the secret of the Christian life.

A poor man of India's low caste once said to Dr. E. Stanley Jones: "Please come and walk through the compound of my humble cottage, and it will be purified of all its impurities and inferiorities!"

Dr. Jones later wrote:

> I knew his faith was misplaced; I couldn't do that! But I knew Jesus could do and did just that. He walks through our minds and spirits and homes, and, lo, life is purified of its impurities and inferiorities. Legend says that where Jesus walked, flowers sprang up in His footsteps. That is legend, but the moral and spiritual equivalent of that does happen. Barrenness breaks into bloom; dead sticks like Aaron's rod begin to bud. The nobodies become somebodies; the ordinary becomes the extraordinary—life begins to live. Dead harps feel the sweep of a Hand and sleeping music is awakened.[1]

---

1. E. Stanley Jones, *Growing Spiritually* (New York: Abingdon Press, 1953), p. 105.

The Resurrection Is the Promise of New Life

Peter went on to say: "You handed him [Jesus] over to be killed, and you disowned him before Pilate, though he had decided to let him go. You disowned the Holy and Righteous One and asked that a murderer be released to you. You killed the author of life, but God raised him from the dead. We are witnesses of this" (Acts 3:13-15).

Being honest with the truth, Peter gave it to them straight. The crowd was guilty of a terrible sin and they knew he was right. They had turned down the Giver of Life and accepted a taker of life—Barabbas for Jesus!

While God is the source of new life, the resurrection of Jesus was His proof that He could keep His promise of new life to all who follow Jesus.

Peter referred to Jesus as the "author of life." Moffatt translates it, "Pioneer of life." The *New English Bible* states it as, "Who has led the way to life." The Greek word means "one who has gone before, who has marked the trail, who has scouted out the unknown and made the passage safe for others to follow." Jesus is the Pioneer of life. He alone has passed through the Resurrection, but it was God's positive proof of eternal life for all who trust in Him. Peter adds, "We are witnesses of this." The Resurrection was attested to by eye-witnesses—enough of them to stand in a court of law! As William LaSor pointed out: "Let us remember this: the apostles did not believe in the Resurrection because it was an article of faith; it became an article of faith because they had seen the risen Lord!"[2]

Vedanayakam Samuel Azariah was the first Anglican bishop of India. Someone asked where one should begin preaching the gospel to those who have never heard it. He

---

2. LaSor, *Church Alive*, p. 61.

answered without hesitation: "You must start from the resurrection of Jesus; what they need to know is that there is a living, loving Saviour, and that He is not far from them."

William Barclay commented: "Without the Resurrection the Church would never have come into being. Had not Jesus risen from the dead, He would have become a memory which would have grown ever fainter and fainter. But the Resurrection was the proof that He was literally indestructible, that He was literally Lord of life and death, that He was literally forever."[3]

Someone has said: "Our faith is rooted in the fact of Christ's resurrection. In His living presence we see that love is stronger than death. Easter does not deny Good Friday, but shows us that death and the grave—though real to our dim eyes—are not the final reality. In this great good news is the power that transforms every dark experience of life into a door of hope." The Resurrection is the promise of more to come!

Faith Is the Condition of New Life

Peter went on to say: "By faith in the name of Jesus, this man whom you see and know was made strong. It is Jesus' name and the faith that comes through him that has given this complete healing to him, as you can all see" (Acts 3:16).

Peter doesn't leave the crowd wondering and worried over their guilt. He moves right into God's answer for the problem of guilt—faith in Jesus! Wholeheartedly trusting in what Jesus did at the Cross as sufficient to cover our sins! We can't understand it—but we can accept it by faith! God reacts to our guilt with love and forgiveness.

---

3. Barclay, *Acts of the Apostles*, p. 30.

Our problem is this: we want to do something to make up for our sins. Trusting sounds too simple—its just not complicated or sophisticated enough to be an adequate answer! So, unfortunately, we decide to try harder!

In a book loaned to me by a parishioner, Charlie Hile, I read:

> Many are willing to commit themselves to a tremendously energetic campaign. They cannot understand why there isn't a one-to-one correlation between effort expended and success achieved. The reason is that the experience of trying involves short-term surface changes. . . . Trying . . . is a matter of forcefully applying more of whatever it is we are already applying. The change is in quantity rather than in quality. . . . Trying is a focused, unrelaxed, unlistening process. . . . They clench their fists, clench their eyes, clench their ears, and clench their feelings. This is why a stalled relationship sometimes starts working the moment we stop trying.
>
> The irony involved in wishing to change oneself is that the only deliberate changes we can count on are the trivial ones. . . . We can, of course, make any conscious choice we care to, but this change will have no staying power.
>
> We can easily switch brands or experiment with a new response or try to carry out some fine intentions, but these are surface changes, outside changes. What we cannot do is design and execute a deep, inside change that involves our own compromise behaviors and unconscious motivations.[4]

The only significant change in our hearts comes by trusting in God! He is our source of new life!

Dwight L. Moody preached a straightforward message on being born again. A woman, who was a busy church worker, waited to speak to him afterward. Angrily,

---

4. Ernst G. Beier and Evans G. Valens, *People Reading* (New York: Stein and Day Publishers, 1975), pp. 110-11.

she said, "Mr. Moody, do you mean to tell me that I, an educated woman, taught from childhood in good ways, and all my life interested in the church, and doing good, must enter heaven the same way as the worst criminals of our day?"

"No, madam," said Moody, "I don't tell you at all: God does. He says everyone who would enter heaven, no matter how good they think they are, or how well educated, or zealous in good works, must be born again."

It's trusting—not trying!

Faith is the condition for receiving new life in Christ. One must learn to rest in the faithfulness of God. One must learn to trust His promise of forgiveness.

It's like the story of two little girls who were counting their coins. One girl added hers: "I have five pennies."

The other lass said: "I have 10."

The first girl replied: "No, you don't. You have only five cents—just like me!"

The second one answered back: "My daddy said he would give me 5 cents when he comes home tonight, so I have 10 cents!"

The Bible says, "Faith is being sure of what we hope for and certain of what we do not see" (Heb. 11:1). Faith is not belief without proof, but trust without reservations. We believe in a thing when we are prepared to act as if it were true!

A young man was serving his first church thousands of miles from his family, his fiancée, and the friends of his school days. He was desperately lonely! His congregation would not follow his leadership due to his youthfulness. In seeking escape from the pressures and finding someone to comfort him, he got involved in a scandal which forced him to leave his church and marry a woman he didn't love.

Overwhelmed by remorse and disgrace, separated

from his church and his chosen vocation, he tried to find a useful place in society, but his heart wasn't in it. The wife with whom he had an empty marriage divorced him, and he couldn't find a job which appealed to him or had any future for him. The poison of deep-seated guilt seeped into all his conscious moments. He was a defeated and broken young man with no hope—no obvious way to recover from his terrible mistake.

In spite of all, his former fiancée believed in him even through the disgrace and divorce. Though she knew all, she married him and gave him a home of real love. His boyhood pastor believed in him and encouraged him to see a pastoral counselor. There he made a clean and complete confession to God. He was able to accept the forgiveness of a loving Heavenly Father. This was the first important step to a new life.

Reviewing the events of his life, acknowledging his mistakes and sins, talking and praying together with his wife and counselor, the young man began to see some light at the end of his dark, dark tunnel of despair. God helped him to see that failures are not irrevocable. In the atmosphere of a loving, caring church fellowship, he had a new start as a person.

Finally, he could hold his head up again and look a person in the eye without cringing. Though he had applied for a job many times in vain, now he began to realize God had forgiven him, that life could open with greater possibilities now. With a sense that God had not deserted him, he gained a growing confidence. One day he became a teacher in a school that really needed him.

The repair work of the brokenhearted begins with trusting God and trusting in the name of Jesus who speaks forgiveness and new life to any who call. Jesus said, "Whoever comes to me I will never drive away" (John 6:37). Faith is the only condition.

Repentance Is the Reception of New Life

Peter, continuing his address at the Temple, admonishes the crowd: "Repent, then, and turn to God" (Acts 3: 19).

Repentance is turning from one's sin and turning toward God. It is a change of direction. It is an inward change of mind, affections, convictions, and commitment. It is a sorrow for sins which turns in faith to God. These men are offered a full and free pardon of the murder of Jesus, and they take hold of it by admitting their sin and turning to God.

Dr. Cyril E. M. Joad was one of the world's great philosophers, but he was a skeptic of Christianity. According to Bill Bright, "Dr. Joad believed that Jesus was only a man, that God was a part of the universe and should the universe be destroyed, God would be destroyed. . . . He believed that there is no such thing as sin, that man was destined for a Utopia. Give man a little time and he will have heaven on earth." His terrible skepticism and unfounded optimism infected many students with atheism.

On one momentous day, though, the *Los Angeles Times* newspaper carried a picture of Dr. Joad with the statement that a dramatic change had taken place in his life. The article told how for many years he had been antagonistic toward Christianity. Whereas he had once denied sin, now he had come to believe that sin was a reality. Two world wars and the imminence of another had demonstrated conclusively to him that man was sinful. Now he believed that the only explanation for sin was found in the Word of God, and the only solution was found in the cross of Jesus Christ. That which he had denied all his life, he now embraced.

Since God made us for fellowship with himself, the Bible calls us back to God and into this fellowship.

Repentance brings about our release from guilt. Peter told the wondering people, "Repent, then, and turn to God, so that your sins may be wiped out" (Acts 3:19). As great as their sin was, it was forgivable! Even though they had murdered Jesus and faced the penalty of eternal death, God extended His mercy toward them: "That your sins may be wiped out!" Jesus had prayed on the Cross for them: "Father, forgive them, for they do not know what they are doing" (Luke 23:34).

Yes, God has a solution to our guilt—wiping away our sins! Our past is cleaned up. William Barclay provides a descriptive note about the phrase "wiped out": "This is a vivid word. Ancient writing was upon papyrus, and the ink used had no acid in it. It therefore did not bite into the papyrus as modern ink does; it simply lay upon the top of it. To erase the writing a man might take a wet sponge and simply wipe it away. So God wipes out the sin of the forgiven man."[5] There are no traces to be read back to us again!

Repentance brings the refreshing of Jesus' presence: "Repent, then, and turn to God, so that your sins may be wiped out, that times of refreshing may come from the Lord" (Acts 3:19-20). That word *refreshing* in the Greek text means "respite" or "relief"! Repentance brings about the relief of God's peace in our minds and hearts! When our sins are wiped out, there comes a relaxation of the soul. No longer is there the torment of guilt and brokenness.

A nervous woman driver whose car had gotten trapped in heavy traffic became hysterical with fear, frustration, and embarrassment. Other drivers frowned at her, honked their horns, and shouted. She was in a helpless condition.

---

5. Barclay, *Acts of the Apostles*, p. 32.

Right then a man stepped from the curb and said, "Lady, if you will move over and let me behind the wheel, I think I can get you out of this mess."

Quickly the calm, skillful driver got the car over to the curb. Traffic unsnarled and flowed freely. The frightened woman regained her control.

When Jesus finds us in a jam, whipped by guilt and failure, chided by our inability to change ourselves, and life seems to be getting unravelled, all He asks is that we let Him take over! He brings the relief we need! He gives strength in our hour of weakness! One must start trusting and quit trying!

Charles Colson, the well-known character from the infamous chapters of Watergate, sat listening to a friend testify about the saving power of Jesus Christ. It was all new to him. With his career collapsing around him, with the ambitions of his life turning to ashes, he drank in the Christian friend's good news. In his own words, he tells what happened:

As I drove out of Tom's driveway, the tears were flowing uncontrollably. There were no streetlights, no moonlight. The car headlights were flooding illumination before my eyes, but I was crying so hard it was like trying to swim under water. I pulled to the side of the road not more than a hundred yards from the entrance to Tom's driveway, the tires sinking into soft mounds of pine needles.

I remember hoping that Tom and Gert wouldn't hear my sobbing, the only sound other than the chirping of crickets that penetrated the still of the night. With my face cupped in my hands, head leaning forward against the wheel, I forgot about machismo, about pretenses, about fears of being weak. And as I did, I began to experience a wonderful feeling of being released. Then came the strange sensation that water was not only running down my cheeks, but surging through my whole body as well, cleansing and cooling as it went. They weren't tears of sadness and remorse, not of joy—but somehow, tears of relief. . . .

And then I prayed my first real prayer. "God, I don't know how to find You, but I'm going to try! I'm not much the way I am now, but somehow I want to give myself to You." I didn't know how to say more, so I repeated over and over the words: Take me.

I had not "accepted" Christ—I still didn't know who He was. My mind told me it was important to find that out first, to be sure that I knew what I was doing, that I meant it and would stay with it. Only, that night, something inside me was urging me to surrender—to what or to whom I did not know.

I stayed there in the car, wet-eyed, praying, thinking, for perhaps half an hour, perhaps longer, alone in the quiet of the dark night. Yet for the first time in my life I was not alone at all.[6]

A few pages later, Colson went off to be alone by the sea, reading the Bible.

And so early that Friday morning, while I sat alone staring at the sea I love, words I had not been certain I could understand or say fell naturally from my lips: "Lord Jesus, I believe You. I accept You. Please come into my life. I commit it to You."

With these few words that morning, while the briny sea churned, came a sureness of mind that matched the depth of feeling in my heart. There came something more: strength and serenity, a wonderful new assurance about life, a fresh perception of myself and the world around me. In the process, I felt old fears, tensions, and animosities draining away. I was coming alive to things I'd never seen before; as if God was filling the barren void I'd known for so many months, filling it to its brim with a whole new kind of awareness.[7]

6. Charles W. Colson, *Born Again* (Old Tappan, N.J.: Fleming H. Revell Company, 1976), pp. 116-17.

7. *Ibid.,* p. 130.

One must learn to quit trying, and begin trusting! He who was nailed to the Cross for our sins is ready to heal and restore one's spirit. The steps to trusting are simple: (1) To acknowledge one's sins to God; (2) to believe God's promise to forgive; (3) to confess Jesus as Savior and Lord of one's life.

The songwriter caught the spirit of this simple trust:

> *Come, every soul by sin oppressed,*
> *There's mercy with the Lord:*
> *And He will surely give you rest*
> *By trusting in His Word.*
>
> *Yes, Jesus is the Truth, the Way*
> *That leads you into rest.*
> *Believe in Him without delay,*
> *And you are fully blest.*
>
> *Only trust Him, only trust Him,*
> *Only trust Him now;*
> *He will save you; He will save you;*
> *He will save you now!*
>
> —JOHN H. STOCKTON

CHAPTER 9

In the Name of Jesus

Acts 4:1-22

A pastor had preached his sermon on Sunday morning about the lame beggar who asked Peter and John for alms, but who was miraculously healed. The lesson from Acts 3 had greatly impressed a little girl in the congregation. Meeting the preacher during the week she said to him "I sure liked your sermon last Sunday."

"Thank you," he replied. "Can you tell me what I preached about?"

"Oh, yes, Sir!" she announced. "Your sermon was all about a man who asked Jesus for *arms* and got legs!"

It's just like Jesus to give abundantly above what we could ask or think! The beggar did get more than he asked for; the healing touch of wholeness—inside and out!

When the crowd of people around the Temple area saw the ex-cripple leaping and praising God, a great swarm of spectators joined the celebration. Having the heart of a preacher, Peter couldn't resist the opportunity to preach to such a gathering. Right on the Temple grounds, people

111

were being converted to Jesus Christ. Someone ran off to tell the authorities about Peter's soapbox sermon. Since it was past six o'clock in the evening, the Temple guards were ordered to put Peter and John in a cellblock until morning.

That's the way the devil works! During a time of great revival and spiritual awakening, there comes a sudden test. This was the first of many arrests and persecutions, which makes the Book of Acts read like a police blotter! The Spirit-filled Church was a society-upsetting influence. It disturbed people. The living Christ was a thorn to the Sadducees.

During Jesus' life and ministry, the Pharisees opposed Him. However, after Jesus drove the money changers out of the Temple, the Sadducees became angry with Him because He threatened their pocketbooks. And now, with Peter preaching about Jesus' resurrection, one of their basic tenets was under attack. The Sadducees didn't believe in life hereafter. For them, the grave was the end of all. Because they didn't believe in the judgment and the resurrection, it was easy for them to be cruel. From their point of view, there was nothing else to answer for! Luke says, "They were greatly disturbed because the apostles were teaching . . . and proclaiming in Jesus the resurrection of the dead" (Acts 4:2). The Greek word for "greatly disturbed" means they were "worked up, indignant, exasperated!" A living religion was a threat to them!

What a vivid contrast! While the religiously liberal leaders sat in their magnificent buildings and appeased the Roman invaders, the people whose religion had caught fire with reality were out on the streets with men who were burdened with the problems of the workaday life.

We must never settle for our routine ceremonies and social groups. To build God's Church, we must be available to Him on the streets of humanity! How else shall our world witness the resurrection of Jesus in the hearts of men and women?

Official religion at the Temple was motivated by fear. But Peter and John were fearlessly motivated by the matchless name of Jesus. While they had no silver or gold, they had ahold of Christ's life and power. It's silly to cling to silver and gold thinking that by so doing, we can ensure the life and power of the Church!

Unlike the Philippian jailer, the Sadducees never bothered to ask, "What must we do to be saved?" They were only concerned with, "What must we do to save face and ensure our jobs?"

The next morning, Annas, Caiaphas, and other leading authorities interrogated Peter and John: "By what power or what name did you do this?" (Acts 4:7).

Peter's answer is found in this statement: "It is by the name of Jesus Christ of Nazareth" (Acts 4:10).

In the Name of Jesus There Is Unconquerable Power

"Then Peter, filled with the Holy Spirit, said to them: 'Rulers and elders of the people! If we are being called to account today for an act of kindness shown to a cripple and are asked how he was healed, then know this, you and everyone else in Israel: It is by the name of Jesus Christ of Nazareth, whom you crucified but whom God raised from the dead, that this man stands before you completely healed. He is "the stone you builders rejected, which has become the capstone." Salvation is found in no one else; for there is no other name under heaven given to men by which we must be saved'" (Acts 4:8-12).

Peter proclaimed Jesus as the Messiah. Being filled with the Spirit, he would not water down his message to the officials by minimizing the Person of Jesus. There's no attempt on Peter's part to be "broadminded" by downgrading Jesus Christ. "Fired by the Spirit, Peter gave a ringing testimony to the uniqueness of Jesus."[1] After all, Jesus was the Messiah, God's own Anointed, His beloved Son. All power was made available to Jesus through God the Father. Peter, in his sermon, portrays Jesus as the Name above every name!

Jesus is the rejected, discarded stone. By quoting Psalm 118, Peter also brought to mind a Jewish tradition concerning the building of Solomon's temple. Ray Stedman tells it well:

> According to Jewish tradition, during the building of the temple a great rock was quarried and shaped by the master mason, but when the builders received it they could find no place to put it. It didn't seem to match any of the blueprints they were working from, so they placed it to one side. After a while because the rock seemed to be in the way, someone pushed it over the edge of a bank and it rolled down into the Kidron Valley and was lost in the bushes. But when the time came to hoist the cornerstone, the great square rock that held everything else in place, no one could seem to find it. The masons sent word that the cornerstone had already been delivered some time earlier, so the on-site builders looked around some more for it, but still no one could seem to find it. Then someone remembered the huge 'extra' rock that had been pushed over the edge. Down they went to the valley, where they found it lying in the bushes. With great effort the builders returned the rejected stone to the temple site and hoisted it into place, where it fit perfectly as the cornerstone of the temple.[2]

Such was the Bible's description of Jesus. He whom God had fashioned before the foundation of the world and had sent to us was rejected: "He was in the world, and though the world was made through him, the world did

---

1. Barker, *They Stood Boldly,* p. 41.
2. Stedman, *Birth of the Body,* p. 83.

not recognize him. He came to that which was his own, but his own did not receive him" (John 1:10-11). And as the Kingdom is being built in the power of the Spirit, Jesus is "the chief cornerstone. In him the whole building is joined together and rises to become a holy temple in the Lord" (Eph. 2:20-21).

Jesus is the One whom they crucified. Those who bow down to this world's materialistic value systems, with the philosophies of might makes right and spiritual anarchy, will always oppose Jesus Christ and hang Him outside as irrelevant, as an interruption, as an intruder.

Jesus is the One whom God raised from the dead. The Father resurrected what men thought they had killed forever. Those Sadducees, like today's sophisticated liberals, rejected the idea of the resurrection. That's why they cling so tenaciously to the trinkets of today. But notice, the Sanhedrin did nothing to disprove the Resurrection of Jesus—except to bribe the guards who saw it! If they could have disproved the Resurrection, there's no doubt they would have done so. When Peter proclaimed Jesus had risen from the dead, they had not one argument—because everyone knew about it.

And Jesus had told them earlier: "Because I live, you also will live" (John 14:19). The open tomb has brought more relief, more joy, more peace of mind than any other announcement mankind ever heard! Just ask anyone who has lost a Christian loved one!

Jesus is the only avenue of salvation. He had said earlier: "I am the way—and the truth and the life. No one comes to the Father except through me" (John 14:6). Peter cut across the grain of popular religion when he said authoritatively, "Salvation is found in no one else; for there is no other name under heaven given to men by which we must be saved" (Acts 4:12).

Such a statement sounds narrow-minded to many ears

115

who are used to hearing: "One religion is as good as another!" But truth is not dependent upon opinions. One religion is not as good as another. One commentator pointed out:

> The practice of child sacrifice is not as good as the care and love for children in Christianity. Nor is the caste system in Hinduism as good as the doctrine of human dignity in Christianity. . . . A man has no choice whether he accepts the law of gravity or not. It is no less valid in the United States as it is in China. His opinions about it may be right or wrong, but the truth stands, regardless of what he thinks about it. Religion is concerned with truth, not opinion.[3]

Jesus is our only way into God's heaven!

During World War II, a pilot was surrounded in the air by several enemy fighter planes. Suddenly, his plane was hit and burst into flames. Though he had been instructed in how to use a parachute, he had never actually jumped with one. In telling the incident to a friend, he said: "I knew I had to jump. I could not pull the string at once because I was surrounded by enemy planes and I had to fall, waiting until I fell into the clouds before pulling the cord."

His friend was amazed, "I don't see how you could do it, never having done it before!"

"I could do it," he answered, "because I knew it was my only chance!"

One had better put his trust in Jesus for entrance into God's kingdom—it is the only way!

Joan of Arc was burned at the stake, accused of being a witch. As the flames leaped around her, she said: "Jesus! Jesus! Jesus!" The passport to heaven is the name of Jesus!

---

3. Buttrick, *Interpreter's Bible*, 9:62.

In the Name of Jesus There Are Undeniable Results

"When they saw the courage of Peter and John and realized that they were unschooled, ordinary men, they were astonished and they took note that these men had been with Jesus. And since they could see the man who had been healed standing there with them, there was nothing they could say. So they ordered them to withdraw from the Sanhedrin and then conferred together. 'What are we going to do with these men?' they asked. 'Everybody living in Jerusalem knows they have done an outstanding miracle, and we cannot deny it. But to stop this thing from spreading any further among the people, we must warn these men to speak no longer to anyone in this name'" (Acts 4:13-17).

Here is the acknowledgment of the miracle. Undeniable results are hard to hide. It's a tough assignment to oppose conclusive evidence!

There's the dynamic of Spirit-filled men. Obviously this man, Peter, was not the cringing coward that he was on the day of crucifixion. He had been filled with instant inspiration by the Holy Spirit. God had invaded him and empowered him. Poise under pressure had not been one of his original assets—but now he was calm and bold. After a night in jail, Peter and John weren't the whimpering country bumpkins the Sanhedrin expected.

The Bible says, "They took note that they had been with Jesus" (Acts 4:13). The Greek word translated "taking note" means "to examine, to watch carefully, to take notes, to weigh action." That's a sobering thought: "The world is always taking notes on you as a Christian, trying to discover the cause of your close relationship with Jesus Christ, and its effectiveness or noneffectiveness in your

117

living."[4] Is there anything in our lives which causes our circle of contacts to wonder if we, too, have been with Jesus?

If it were illegal to be a born-again Christian today, and you were on trial, would there be enough evidence to convict you?

The Bible also says, "They saw the courage of Peter and John" (Acts 4:13). Their courage or boldness means in classical Greek, "freedom of speech, plainness, openness, confidence"! One of the areas where people will take note of our relationship with Christ is in our moral courage!

John Jasper, a great Black preacher, used to begin his sermons with the statement: "I'm here on my iron legs to preach God's Holy Word!" Such boldness and courage gain a hearing.

Too many Christians speak of their religious convictions as though they have both feet "planted firmly in the air!" And you can never lift this old world very much in that position. One must get his feet planted on the Solid Rock, Christ Jesus. One needs to become a convict of a great miracle of grace.

There's the dynamic of the Spirit-healed man. It was an unanswerable fact. Kenneth Taylor paraphrases it vividly: "The Council could hardly discredit the healing when the man they had healed was standing right there beside them!" (Acts 4:14, TLB). One can almost see a Sadducee arguing with Peter trying to discredit the miracle, but the ex-crippled beggar keeps pacing back and forth walking between them, obstructing his view of the opponent! It's really difficult to argue against Christianity when you've got a living, walking, talking evidence all around you!

4. Louis H. Evans, *Life's Hidden Power* (Westwood, N.J.: Fleming H. Revell Company, 1958), p. 87.

118

After sending Peter and John out of the Council chambers, the honesty of the Sanhedrin was even more candid: "Everybody living in Jerusalem knows they have done an outstanding miracle, and we cannot deny it" (Acts 4:16). The Greek text of verse 14 is even more vivid: "They kept on having nothing to say against it!"

No wonder everyone was amazed—the lame man was past 40 years of age. Surely he was a hopeless case! Miracles never happen to a man that old, do they? But the power of God is unlimited. And even though a man is shackled to his sins for more than 50 years, and even though sociologists dismiss him as hopeless, and even though psychologists give up on him—still God can save an old brokenhearted sinner! God can set that man's mind and soul at ease!

There's the dynamic of spiritual births! One can't put much stock in miracles that have no effects. But this miraculous cure did something in the hearts and imaginations of spiritually hungry people. So many were added to the kingdom of God that Luke tells us there were now about 5,000 men who were believers. Since there were so many, they only counted the men—the number of households! These were undeniable results of the unconquerable power of Jesus' name!

Spiritual conversions are hard to explain away. It's hard to convince a man who has been born again that there is nothing to it. He has tasted and found that the Lord is good!

Two atheists traveling on a train many years ago were discussing Jesus' life. One of them said, "I think an interesting romance could be written about Jesus."

The other replied: "And you are just the man to write it. Set forth the correct view of His life and character. Tear down the prevailing sentiment about His deity and paint Him like He was—a man among men."

The suggestion was taken and the man began his study and wrote the romantic novel. The man who challenged him to the project was Colonel Robert Ingersoll; the author was General Lew Wallace; and the book was *Ben Hur*. However, in the process of working on the life of Jesus, Lew Wallace faced the undeniable results! The more he studied the life of Jesus and His invincible character, the more he became profoundly convinced that Jesus was more than a man among men.

At last, like the centurion at the Cross, Lew Wallace met the unconquerable power of Jesus' name and cried, "Surely this man was the Son of God!" (Mark 15:39). Lew Wallace met Christ face-to-face.

In the Name of Jesus There Is Unsuppressible Good News

"Then they called them in again and commanded them not to speak or teach at all in the name of Jesus. But Peter and John replied, 'Judge for yourselves whether it is right in God's sight to obey you rather than God. For we cannot help speaking about what we have seen and heard'" (Acts 4:18-20).

Here is the presenting of the message! As William Barclay put it, "They could not very well execute Peter and John for bringing health and healing to a lame man; there was no possible charge or crime there; so they compromised. They let them go but they laid down one condition—that they would never again preach or teach about Jesus."[5]

Peter responded: "We cannot but speak the things which we have seen and heard" (Acts 4:20, KJV).

---

5. William Barclay, *God's Young Church* (Philadelphia: The Westminster Press, 1970), p. 28.

We have an unsuppressible truth. Jesus can salvage men and women. That's too good to keep quiet about! God never looks at people as hopeless.

A man, with a surgeon friend, toured the doctor's hospital. As they went into the rooms and wards, the visitor was overwhelmed with the injured, sick, and dying. He heard the pitiful sounds of a crying child, sick and lonely. The moans of someone coming out of anesthetic drifted through the halls. He finally said to his friend, the surgeon: "I don't see how you can take it—seeing people suffer, listening to their complaints—and you seem happy and cheerful right in the midst of all this."

The physician said with a smile: "If we did not see all sickness from the curative standpoint, we couldn't stand it. But we look at every case as one we can either cure or help alleviate the suffering. That's why it is less hard for us."

And that is how Jesus sees sinners—not from how bad they are, but from the curative viewpoint: what He is able to do for them, if they will let Him. That's why Jesus went to the Cross for our suffering and sin. How else could He stand bearing our sins on the Cross? He looks at us with an eye to what He can do in us if we will surrender to Him. Jesus can salvage the hopeless, brokenhearted, despairing ones who come to Him.

We have an unsuppressible love! It is a love which must be expressed or be quenched! When warned to stop using Jesus' name, Peter said, "We cannot but speak." The Greek text expresses it this way: "We are *not* able *not* to speak." It's like a fountain which cannot be capped! It must flow out! These men couldn't give in to outward pressure because of the pressure on the inside—conscience, honesty, responsibility. But more than all of these was the power of love.

Inner constraints are more powerful than outer restraints. Barclay graphically illustrated this truth:

> In the days of the Reformation, Martin Luther was summoned to the town of Worms to answer for his faith. He was only a humble monk with no place or power or influence. He was told that if he went he would have to meet the greatest men in the Roman Catholic Church and that if they got him into their power it would go ill with him. He answered, "I would go to Worms if there were as many devils there as there are tiles on the housetops." He was told that if he went Duke George would oppose him and arrest him. "I would go," he said, "if it rained Duke Georges."[6]

Peter said, "Judge for yourselves whether it is right in God's sight to obey you rather than God" (Acts 4:19). Surely, it was an impressive moment as they stood before that semicircle of scowling faces. After all, these were the same men who had condemned Jesus to death only a few weeks before! However, Jesus had instructed the disciples: "If you love me, you will obey me!" They had already made their choice to go with Jesus. Since they had an utter loyalty to Jesus, what men commanded them meant very little!

During a battle between the English and Dutch navies, the English had taken a terrible beating, but wouldn't quit. The Dutch leader, De Witt, later gave tribute to the English navy: "English sailors may be killed, but they cannot be conquered."[7]

"We cannot but speak the things which we have seen and heard"—we have an unsuppressible personal knowledge. We have the defense of personal experience with Jesus Christ. That is why second-hand religion won't stand the tests of life. What we have experienced we cannot keep

---

6. *Ibid.*, p. 29.
7. *Ibid.*, p. 30.

to ourselves. What we have seen God work in us and through us is a spring of assurance.

A young Chinese Christian was coming to America to study in one of our universities. A passenger next to him on the train noticed he was reading a Bible. Getting into a conversation with the Chinese youth, the passenger tried to put doubt into his mind about the validity of the Bible. But, then, he added: "I wouldn't want to disturb your faith in Christ, however."

The Chinese replied, "Sir, if you could disturb my faith in Christ, He would not be a big enough Savior for me!"

We have an unsuppressible joy! Having tried insults, innuendo, and intimidation, the authorities threatened them. Threatening is a cheap substitute for a reasonable argument. So they let Peter and John go. The Bible says, "For all men glorified God for that which was done" (Acts 4:21, KJV). *The Living Bible* paraphrases it: "For everyone was praising God for this wonderful miracle!" They kept on praising God, even while the Sanhedrin threatened Peter and John. This unsuppressible joy laughs at the helplessness of God's enemies. The victory has been won in Christ Jesus. Darkness can never extinguish the tiny flame of a single candle. Ours is a joy of victory!

In the name of Jesus there is unconquerable power!

In the name of Jesus there are undeniable results!

In the name of Jesus there is unsuppressible Good News!

The captain of the ironclad ship *Merrimac* was a skeptic of the Christian faith. After his retirement, the years passed until he became a resident of the Pennsylvania Soldiers' Home.

One day he argued with the chaplain against salvation. But the chaplain challenged the old seaman:

"Captain, take this Bible and read it carefully. Mark in red anything you don't believe."

With a sparkle in his eyes, the old captain accepted the challenge.

As the days passed, the chaplain would drop in the captain's room and ask if he had marked anything in red. But the old man would only grin, never saying a word. One day the chaplain opened the door, he found the body of the old captain on his bed. He had died during the night. The Bible was open nearby, so the chaplain leafed through it to see how many passages had been marked in red. Not one was found. However, when he came to John 3:16, he found these words written on the margin: "I have cast my anchor in a safe harbor, thank God!"

Through the unconquerable power of Jesus' name, all his doubts had been swept aside. His sins were washed away. He had found the message of unsuppressible Good News!

That Name still lives, and will live on forever;
Though kings and kingdoms will forgotten be,
Through mists or rain, 'twill be beclouded never;
That Name shall shine, and shine eternally!
—OSCAR C. ELIASON

CHAPTER 10

Birds of a Feather

Acts 4:23-33

During World War II, there was only one U.S. Regiment in Burma. Its peculiar name was "The 5,307th Composite Unit." Three battalions of the unit were cut off for months behind Japanese lines. In the steamy jungles, these men felt like a forgotten handful of disease-ridden troops facing impossible odds. During one long night, pinned down under sniper fire, in the rain and without food, one G.I. mumbled, "Where are the 5,306 *other* composite units?"[1]

Both soldiers and Christians need the support of others. Believe it! There's a sense of loneliness out there when one is facing tough opposition. Sometimes a fellow wonders, "Where are all the *other* Christians?"

Peter and John had already tasted the firstfruits of persecution. These early beginnings of threat would ripen into persecution and martyrdom. Luke tells us, "On their release, Peter and John went back to their own people"

---

1. Barker, *They Stood Boldly*, p. 45.

(Acts 4:23). When the pressure is on, what kind of friends do you go to? When the restraints are taken off, what kind of company do you seek? A proverbial saying puts it:

Birds of a feather
Flock together!

Some people look for a castle. They want some temptation-proof fortress. They strive to live in a one-room soundproof castle insulated from the pressures of life.

Some people look for a temporary camp. Wanting no stakes driven down, no roots, no permanent relationships or responsibilities, they are lured into the vagabond life, continually on the move. Too many folk have "gone west" to avoid personal attachments. Flocking to the great cities, they want to do as they please in the anonymous metropolitan masses.

Some people look for a cloister. They think religion is an island of personal concern. For them the ideal is withdrawal from the realities of human need and compassion. They are convinced that Christian separateness means isolation whereas the Bible teaches insulation.

Peter and John, however, looked for the community of believers. Into this fellowship, the Holy Spirit brought revival and refreshing. Little did they know that up ahead was an era of persecution and trial. A recent statement caught the writer's attention: Great revivals precede, not follow, periods of great persecution! God knew these people would need a revival to prepare them for the future.

After being released, Peter and John went to their friends. What happened? How did the believers help and strengthen each other?

It Was in a Great Season of United Prayer

The Bible says, "On their release, Peter and John went back to their own people and reported all that the chief priests and elders had said to them. When they heard this, they raised their voices together in prayer to God" (Acts 4:23-24).

Persecution drove them to prayer. The disciples didn't react to the persecution and threats with anger or revenge. The best way to meet opposition is to pray. When passing through some dark spot, learn to pray instead of worry! I saw a bumper sticker which said: "Why pray when you can worry!"

"They raised their voices together in prayer to God!" It was none of that soft, monotone, fluffy, half-embarrassed monologue that passes for prayer these days! Most of us have been in prayer meetings that were so dull it was obvious no one wanted to talk to God. What's this hang-up about prayer? Some people are so timid, they can't even lead in silent prayer!

But not the prayer meeting in Acts 4. Those people prayed out loud in "one accord" (Acts 4:24, KJV). The English word for "symphony" comes from "one accord." It's a disgrace to hear a great symphony orchestra fussing around with little squeaky notes when they ought to join together in a sweep of sound with power and harmony that seems like heaven's music.

Too many times people are through praying when they ought to be praying through! If it's big enough to talk about, it is big enough to pray about!

The disciples prayed a prayer of praise! Apparently all joined with Peter in reciting Psalm 2, one of the songs known from memory. It is the earliest recorded utterance of praise in the Christian Church. In spite of threats, they had a song instead of a sob!

The prayer of praise began: "'Sovereign Lord . . . you made the heaven and the earth and the sea, and everything in them'" (Acts 4:24). Addressing themselves to the Lord, they used a more uncommon Greek word for "Lord." They used *despotes* from which we get our English word, *despot*. It means, "Absolute Master of the universe; unrestricted power." Coming away from the tiny tyranny of men, the apostles prayed to their Omnipotent, Sovereign Creator. After all, He is still in charge! He is still on the throne! He is still in control of the march of history! Persecutions and pressures just underscore the Lordship of God. We can praise Him even in the storms. Like the great Aeolian harps strung between castle towers are silent until the storm rages—then the music sings above the blast.

The disciples prayed a prayer centered in Jesus: "'You spoke by the Holy Spirit through the mouth of your servant, our father David: "Why do the nations rage, and the people plot in vain? The kings of the earth take their stand, and the rulers gather together against the Lord and against his Anointed One." Indeed Herod and Pontius Pilate met together with the Gentiles and the people of Israel in this city to conspire against your holy servant Jesus, whom you anointed. They did what your power and will had decided beforehand should happen'" (Acts 4:25-28).

Jesus is the reality of our prayers. His is the only name in which we can pray to the Father.

Leo Tolstoy told of a man who was on a hunting trip with his brother. At his bedside, he knelt in prayer. When he finished, his brother said, "Are you still doing that?" Nothing else was said—but that man's prayer life was demolished. Tolstoy wrote, "His brother's words were like the push of a finger against a wall ready to tumble over with its own weight." His faith was only an empty form.

Many go through meaningless ritual. Nothing happens when they pray because they don't expect anything to happen. If they quit praying it wouldn't change anything for them. Prayer is not a form, an exercise, a ritual. Prayer is atuning our wills with Jesus. He is the focal point of prayer. Prayer is conversation with Jesus who is a present Friend in time of need. He is not an "absentee designer" or "a retired chairman of the board." God became real as the Holy Spirit revealed Jesus in the Scriptures. The apostles acknowledged that Jesus was God's meeting place with man.

The disciples prayed a prayer of enablement. Prosperity has often been fatal to the Church, but persecution never has! One Russian commissar complained: "Religion is like a nail. The harder you hit it, the deeper it goes into the wood!"

They prayed, "Now, Lord, consider their threats and enable your servants to speak your word with great boldness" (Acts 4:29). Those Christians realized that the opposition was against God—not just against them. Persecution had come because they represented Jesus—and it had not taken God by surprise. He knew and understood.

One of the papal ambassadors threatened Martin Luther, suggesting he would soon be deserted by all his followers: "Where would you be then?"

Luther answered, "Right where I am now—in the hands of God!"

Jesus has said: "No servant is greater than his master. If they persecuted me, they will persecute you also" (John 15:20). He had also taught them: "Blessed are you when people insult you, persecute you and falsely say all kinds of evil against you because of me. Rejoice and be glad, because great is your reward in heaven" (Matt. 5:11-12). As they prayed, these disciples were sensing the blessing of God. They were praising God and leaping for joy. They didn't ask for the persecution to end. They asked for strength to endure. Peter and John didn't pray for deliverance from hardship, but they asked for *boldness*—deliverance from fear or cowardice: "Enable your servants to speak your word with great boldness!"

One should not pray for lighter burdens, but for stronger backs! The great preacher of Boston, Phillips Brooks, said: "Do not pray for tasks equal to your powers. Pray for powers equal to your tasks!"

The disciples prayed a prayer for the unusual: "Stretch out your hand to heal and perform miraculous signs and wonders through the name of your holy servant Jesus" (Acts 4:30). The band of Christians needed miracles of grace and they knew it! But they also knew God was able! We have not, because we ask not.

Those early Christians strengthened and supported one another in a great season of united prayer.

It Was in a Great Atmosphere of Expectancy

"After they prayed, the place where they were meeting was shaken. And they were all filled with the Holy Spirit and spoke the word of God boldly" (Acts 4:31). In response to their great season of united prayer, God began to work among them. Things began to happen.

First, the place was shaken! When people pray to God believing, there's a climate of expectancy that is electrifying and dynamic. Anything can happen to a crowd like that! Suddenly it seemed the whole place was shaken up. It throbbed with power too great to be contained! It may have been an earthquake, but, after all, God is big enough to shake the world—He made it in the first place.

Ray Stedman noted: "This was God's symbolic answer to the disciples' prayer. He was saying to them, in a figurative way, that He would shake Jerusalem and the world by the message these disciples were proclaiming."[2]

Mark Moore tells of a minor earthquake which shook a church in which some of the old saints were meeting. As

---

2. Stedman, *Birth of the Body,* p. 93.

the tremors began, they fell on their knees and started praying in desperation. They were anxious to get things straightened out with God—just in case! But, when the earthquake stopped, the old saints stopped praying and climbed back up into the pews.

The faithful custodian, watching the event, said, "O Lord, shake 'em again! Shake 'em again!"

My prayer for our own denomination is: "O Lord, shake us again! Shake us again! Don't ever again let us settle down into the comfortable pew, the social elite, the church without a mission, the form without the power of the Holy Spirit. O God, shake us again!"

Second, the people were filled with the Holy Spirit! Many of that crowd were on hand at the Feast of Pentecost several weeks previous. The Holy Spirit had baptized them with His sanctifying power. While there is one baptism of the Spirit, there are many fillings! New pressures and new crises arose, and God filled His people anew and afresh with His power of enablement. Here was a mighty outpouring of the Spirit to give added strength in the midst of trial. It's revival! It's renewal! Call it whatever seems good, but God was stirring in their hearts, giving vitality and power to His Church!

The church today needs that brokenness, freshness, radiance which comes from revival.

A couple were vacationing in Florida. The husband who was out swimming got into trouble. The lifeguard rescued him and brought him up on the beach swarming with spectators. The wife heard the lifeguard say: "I think we should give him artificial respiration."

She interrupted, "Oh, don't use the artificial! I can afford the real thing!"

And, it's the real thing that the church needs today. Let the Spirit of God bring us back to the normalcy of Pentecost!

Spirit of the living God,
Fall fresh on me.
Melt me; mold me;
Fill me; use me!
Spirit of the living God,
Fall fresh on me!

—DANIEL IVERSON

Third, the promise of God was boldly proclaimed! Peter and John and the others had prayed that they might "with all boldness go on speaking [God's] word." Having defied the Sanhedrin, they asked for the courage to live up to their words. In that great atmosphere of expectancy, God answered their prayer. Possessed by the Holy Spirit, those men spoke with boldness, meaning, "without inhibition!" God can deliver us from our paralyzing fears, our timidities which hinder His work through us! God did it in Acts 4 and He will do it today!

The early Christians supported one another in a great season of united prayer resulting in a great atmosphere of expectancy!

It Was in a Great Fellowship of Unity

"All the believers were one in heart and mind. No one claimed that any of his possessions was his own, but they shared everything they had. With great power the apostles continued to testify to the resurrection of the Lord Jesus, and much grace was with them all" (Acts 4:32-33).

Differences of opinion had not separated them. They were one in the bond of love! Divisions and barriers had not been erected. They were glad to take part in the family of God.

That kind of unity is too often missing today. A young Methodist pastor had been asked to conduct the funeral of

132

a prominent Baptist layman whose family was at odds with their own pastor. Not knowing what was ethical, he wired the bishop for instructions. The bishop wired back: "Bury all the Baptists you can!"

The Early Church had a fellowship of common belief: "All the believers." Common belief was the basis for fellowship: belief in the crucified Christ as God's provision for sin and forgiveness, and belief in the resurrected Christ as God's provision for eternal life. Their foundation was built on God's fundamentals. That is what tied them together.

The great Pacific Coast redwood trees are the tallest trees in the world. Some of them are 300 feet high and more than 2,500 years old. Most other trees have a root system which goes as deep as the tree is tall. But not the redwoods! Their root systems are dependent upon the surface water of rainfall. Since their roots are so shallow, one finds them growing only in groves. The roots of all the trees in the grove intertwine, locking themselves together. Redwoods can withstand the storms because they are not standing alone. They support and protect each other.

Christians share their "roots" by common dependency upon Jesus! Our unity begins in our common beliefs.

The Early Church had a fellowship of shared commitment. "All the believers were one in heart and mind" (Acts 4:32). Intellectually and emotionally the disciples were in harmony. They not only believed the same basic truths, but they felt about it with the same intensity of commitment.

Ray Stedman has commented:

> They emotionally enjoyed their unity. It was part of their daily life. In many churches today there is unity, a oneness of spirit, but there is no experience of it in the soul. It is quite possible to come to church and

133

sit together in the pews, united in a physical presence with other Christians, or to sing the same hymns and listen to the same message and be related to God individually, but to have no sense of body life, no sense of belonging to one another.[3]

Christians are not always going to agree, but there can be a unity of love, of belonging together. In the Early Church the members were moved by a unity of common commitment to Jesus Christ. The unity of Christians ought to be fulfilled by an answer given by Aristotle long ago. He was asked, "What is a friend?"

He replied, "One soul dwelling in two bodies!"

Being of one heart and mind was illustrated by Fletcher Galloway: "One of the British soldiers, who survived the tragic ordeal of Dunkirk, was asked how he felt as he was going through it. 'What did it feel like,' his friend inquired, 'to be on the beach of Dunkirk with the raging sea in front of you, the German armies and their tanks crowding in behind you, and the German bombers roaring overhead?'

"The soldier replied, 'It was a strange feeling I had. I felt that every one of those 200,000 men around me was my brother and would give his life for me and I would give my life for him. We were all in it together, and I felt that somehow we were going to make it through.'"

The Early Church had a fellowship of spontaneous generosity. "No one claimed that any of his possessions was his own, but they shared everything they had" (Acts 4:32). They became more interested in people than possessions! Personal possessions became possessions with a purpose. Spontaneous generosity toward each other marked them different from the world which scratched its head saying, "Behold, how they love one another!" The fullness

---

3. *Ibid.*, pp. 96-97.

of the Holy Spirit brought them a sense of responsibility toward each other, a sensitiveness to the needs of a brother in Christ!

This kind of sharing was not enforced nor legislated. It was a spontaneous generosity which has marked the Christian community. These expressions were over and above their tithes which they paid faithfully at the Temple during the hour of worship. Tithe belongs to God; but the offerings came as their hearts were moved to give and share! Unlike the alms customarily given to beggars, this sharing was given to brothers in Christ who were in particular need.

Charles Spurgeon sent a letter to a young fellow: "God bless you. Enclosed is a check for 10 pounds."

The grateful young man wrote back: "Thank you, Dr. Spurgeon, for your letter and good wishes, and particularly for the practical application of them!" Let's not forget the practical application of our unity in Christ.

The Early Church had a fellowship of anointed witness. "With great power the apostles continued to testify to the resurrection of the Lord Jesus" (Acts 4:33). The King James Version translates: "With great power gave the apostles witness of the resurrection." The Greek verb for "gave" suggests the idea of giving what was due, of paying back a debt. We owe it to Jesus to give our testimony of what He has done in our lives. Such a testimony is accompanied by power! The disciples witnessed to the Resurrection and it was so effective it bore results!

The resurrection of Jesus was the necessary proof of His ability to keep His promises. Since Jesus offers life, a church ought to be a resurrection center—a place where hope is resurrected, where the unity of love for one another is resurrected, where the offer of a new start is resurrected!

The Early Church had a fellowship of undeserved worth! "Much grace was with them all" (Acts 4:33). A sense of total dependence upon the grace of God brings a oneness to God's people. How often any one of us has had occasion to admit, "There, but for the grace of God, go I"! Since all have sinned and come short of God's glory, there's but the thin line of grace which separates the sinner and saint! We can make no claim to righteousness of our own. *Grace is God's riches at Christ's expense!*

On October 19, 1977, I heard Stuart Briscoe preach in Banff, Alberta, Canada. In that great message, he gave three definitions:

Justice: "We get what we deserve."
Mercy: "We don't get all that we deserve."
Grace: "We get what we don't deserve."

Yes, grace is what has brought us together. Grace has given us what we need but don't deserve! God's grace has given spiritual life to those who were spiritually dead! And now we are *not* worthless! Our value is based on the price of redemption. We are no longer worms, but sons and daughters of the King of kings and Lord of lords! We are now worth a King's ransom—and don't ever forget it!

When Bill Carle, the opera singer, was converted, his friends in the entertainment world turned away from him. One night in a great evangelistic service, he gave his testimony through word and song.

As he came to the dramatic climax, he said: "Some people ask me: Don't you miss hobnobbing with the stars of the stage?"

As he answered this question he took his red Bible in his hand and lifted it skyward. "I *am* associating with the stars," he said. "The stars I used to know will go to a Christless grave. But I have many new stars to take their place." Then his magnificent voice sounded forth:

> *"We shall shine as the stars of the morning,*
> *With Jesus, the Crucified One.*

We shall rise to be like Him forever,
Eternally shine as the sun."[4]

In the face of persecution and trials, Peter and John joined with their friends in a great season of united prayer. They basked in a great atmosphere of expectancy. They shared a great fellowship of unity.

It's my prayer that God's people today will give the same kind of help and support to one another as we look for and work for the coming of Jesus Christ.

In his book *Living God's Will*, Dwight L. Carlson related a story told by a physician, Dr. Haddon W. Robinson.

On New Year's Day, 1929, the Georgia Tech football team played in the Rose Bowl against the University of California. During the first half, a player from "Cal" named Roy Riegels recovered a fumble and ran with the ball—in the wrong direction! Luckily, a teammate caught him and tackled him just before he crossed the wrong goal line.

Georgia Tech, however, finally got the ball and scored—that touchdown became the margin of victory. When halftime came, everyone murmured: "What will coach Nibbs Price do with Roy Riegels in the second half of the game?"

The team from the University of California filed into the dressing room at halftime and sat in silence. Riegels put a blanket around his shoulders and sat in a corner, put his face in his hands, and cried like a baby.

Usually the coach has a lot to talk about with his team during the halftime break—but this time Coach Price was silent. No doubt he was trying to think how to handle the awkward situation and trying to decide what to do with

---

4. Mendell Taylor, *Every Day with the Psalms* (Kansas City: Beacon Hill Press of Kansas City, 1972), p. 224.

Riegels. The signal came indicating it was time to return to the playing field. The coach interrupted the strange silence saying simply: "Men, the same team that played the first half will start the second half."

The players got up and went out—all but Roy Riegels. He didn't budge. The coach called back to him: "Roy, didn't you hear me? The same team that played the first half will start the second half!"

With tears running down his cheeks, that strong football player said: "Coach, I can't do it to save my life. I've disgraced you. I've disgraced the University of California. I've ruined myself. I couldn't face that crowd in the stadium to save my life!"

Coach Price reached out and put his hands on Riegels' shoulders and said: "Roy, get up and go on back. The game is only half over!"

Roy Riegels went back and played the whole game. Even the Georgia Tech players said they never saw a man play football as Roy did in that second half.[5]

Having read that beautiful story, I, too, said: "What a coach!" And as we have studied how God took Peter and John and the others, giving them encouragement and power, I cannot help but exclaim, "What a God!"

Sometimes we run the ball in the wrong direction. We stumble and fall flat and are so ashamed of ourselves that we never want to try again. But God comes to us in our hour of brokenness, and bends over us, saying: "Get up and go on back. The game of life is only half over!"

The gospel of grace is the Good News of a second chance, a third chance, a whole new beginning! God, our Comforter and Encourager, will never leave us nor forsake us!

---

5. Dwight L. Carlson, *Living God's Will* (Old Tappan, N.J.: Fleming H. Revell Company, 1976), pp. 16-17.

When at the golden portals I am standing,
   All my tribulations, all my sorrows past,
How sweet to hear the blessed proclamation,
   "Enter, faithful servant, welcome home at last."

"I will not forget thee or leave thee,
   In my hands I'll hold thee;
   In my arms I'll fold thee.
I will not forget thee or leave thee;
I am thy Redeemer; I will care for thee."

—CHARLES H. GABRIEL

Bibliography

Airhart, Arnold E. *Beacon Bible Expositions,* Vol. 5. Kansas City: Beacon Hill Press of Kansas City, 1977.

Alford, Henry. *The New Testament for English Readers.* Chicago: Moody Press, n.d.

Arnold, Milo L. *The Christian Adventure.* Kansas City: Beacon Hill Press of Kansas City, 1974.

Barclay, William. *God's Young Church.* Philadelphia: The Westminster Press, 1970.

_____. *The Acts of the Apostles;* The Daily Study Bible. Philadelphia: The Westminster Press, 1953.

_____. *The Gospel of Luke;* The Daily Study Bible. Philadelphia: The Westminster Press, 1953.

_____: *The Mind of Jesus.* New York: Harper and Brothers, 1960.

_____. *The Promise of the Spirit.* Philadelphia: The Westminster Press, 1960.

Barker, William P. *They Stood Boldly.* Westwood, N.J.: Fleming H. Revell Company, 1967.

Beier, Ernst G., and Valens, Evans G. *People Reading.* New York: Stein and Day Publishers, 1975.

Benner, Hugh C. *The Church in Mission.* Kansas City: Beacon Hill Press of Kansas City, 1976.

Benson, Joseph. *Benson's Commentary,* Vol. 4. New York: T. Mason and G. Lane, 1839.

Blair, Edward P. *The Acts and Apocalyptic Literature.* New York: Abingdon-Cokesbury Press, 1956.

Bruce, F. F. "Commentary on the Book of the Acts"; *The New International Commentary on the New Testament.* Grand Rapids: Wm. B. Eerdmans Publishing Company, 1976.

Butt, Howard. *The Velvet-Covered Brick.* New York: Harper and Row, Publishers, 1973.

Buttrick, George Arthur, editor. *The Interpreter's Bible,* Vol. 9. New York: Abingdon Press, 1954.

Carlson, Dwight L. *Living God's Will.* Old Tappan, N.J.: Fleming H. Revell Company, 1976.

141

Carnahan, Roy E. *Creative Pastoral Management*. Kansas City: Beacon Hill Press of Kansas City, 1976.

Carter, Charles W., and Earle, Ralph. *The Evangelical Commentary on the Acts of the Apostles*. Grand Rapids: Zondervan Publishing House, 1959.

Carver, William Owen. *The Acts of the Apostles*. Nashville: Broadman Press, 1916.

Clarke, Adam. *Clarke's Commentary*, Vol. 5. New York: Abingdon Press, n.d.

Colson, Charles W. *Born Again*. Old Tappan, N.J.: Fleming H. Revell Company, 1976.

Davidson, F., editor. *The New Bible Commentary*. Grand Rapids: Wm. B. Eerdmans Publishing Company, 1958.

Ellicott, Charles John. *A Bible Commentary for English Readers*, Vol. 7. London: Cassell and Company, Ltd., n.d.

Evans, Louis H. *Life's Hidden Power*. Westwood, N.J.: Fleming H. Revell Company, 1958.

Fallis, William J. *Studies in Acts*. Nashville: Broadman Press, 1949.

Greathouse, William M. *The Fullness of the Spirit*. Kansas City: Nazarene Publishing House, 1958.

Henry, Carl F. H., editor. *The Biblical Expositor*, Vol. 3. Philadelphia: A. J. Holman Company, 1960.

Henry, Matthew. *Matthew Henry's Commentary*, Leslie F. Church, editor. Grand Rapids: Zondervan Publishing House, 1961.

Hervey, A. C. "The Acts of the Apostles," *The Pulpit Commentary*, Vol. 1. H. D. M. Spence and Joseph S. Exell, editors. London: Funk and Wagnalls Company, 1908.

Huttenlocker, Keith. *Love Makes the Word Go Round*. Anderson, Ind.: Warner Press, 1974.

Jones, E. Stanley. *Growing Spiritually*. New York: Abingdon Press, 1953.

_____. *The Way to Power and Poise*. New York: Abingdon-Cokesbury Press, 1949.

LaSor, William Sanford. *Church Alive*. Glendale, Calif.: Regal Books Division, G/L Publications, 1972.

Lee, Robert G. *Great Is the Lord.* Westwood, N.J.: Fleming H. Revell Company, 1955.

Luccock, Halford E. *Marching off the Map.* New York: Harper and Brothers, Publishers, 1952.

Mayfield, Joseph H., and Earle, Ralph. *Beacon Bible Commentary,* Vol. 7. Kansas City: Beacon Hill Press of Kansas City, 1965.

Miller, Keith. *The Taste of New Wine.* Waco, Tex.: Word Books, 1965.

Morgan, G. Campbell. *An Exposition of the Whole Bible.* Westwood, N.J.: Fleming H. Revell Company, 1959.

———. *The Acts of the Apostles.* Westwood, N.J.: Fleming H. Revell Company, 1924.

Phillips, J. B. *Letters to Young Churches.* New York: The Macmillan Company, 1956.

Purkiser, W. T.; Taylor, Richard S.; and Taylor, Willard H. *God, Man, and Salvation.* Kansas City: Beacon Hill Press of Kansas City, 1977.

Robertson, Archibald Thomas. *Word Pictures in the New Testament,* Vols. 2-3. Nashville: Broadman Press, 1930.

Seamands, John T. *On Tiptoe with Love.* Kansas City: Beacon Hill Press of Kansas City, 1971.

Snyder, Howard A. *The Problem of Wine Skins.* Downers Grove, Ill.: Inter-Varsity Press, 1975.

Spruce, Fletcher Clarke. *When God Comes.* Kansas City: Beacon Hill Press, 1950.

Stedman, Ray C. *Birth of the Body.* Santa Ana, Calif.: Vision House Publishers, 1974.

Taylor, Mendell. *Every Day with the Psalms.* Kansas City: Beacon Hill Press of Kansas City, 1972.

Thomas, W. H. Griffith. *Outline Studies in the Acts of the Apostles.* Grand Rapids: Wm. B. Eerdmans Publishing Company, 1956.

Townsend, Robert. *Up the Organization.* New York: Alfred A. Knopf, 1970

Wells, H. G. *The Outline of History,* Vol. 2. Garden City, N.Y.: Garden City Books, 1956.